Francis Pigou, Francis Pigou

Faith and Practice

A Selection of Sermons Preached in St. Philip's Chapel, Regent Street

.

Francis Pigou, Francis Pigou

Faith and Practice
A Selection of Sermons Preached in St. Philip's Chapel, Regent Street

ISBN/EAN: 9783743427556

Manufactured in Europe, USA, Canada, Australia, Japa

Cover: Foto ©Lupo / pixelio.de

Manufactured and distributed by brebook publishing software (www.brebook.com)

Francis Pigou, Francis Pigou

Faith and Practice

Faith and Practice;

A SELECTION

OF

SERMONS,

PREACHED IN

ST. PHILIP'S CHAPEL, REGENT STREET.

BY

FRANCIS PIGOU, M.A., F.R.G.S.,

INCUMBENT.

London,

RIVINGTONS, WATERLOO PLACE;

| HIGH STREET, | TRINITY STREET, |
| Oxford. | Cambridge. |

1865.

LONDON:

GILBERT AND RIVINGTON, PRINTERS
ST. JOHN'S SQUARE.

TO

HER ROYAL HIGHNESS

THE DUCHESS OF CAMBRIDGE,

IN

GRATEFUL ACKNOWLEDGMENT

OF

MANY KINDNESSES,

THIS

VOLUME OF SERMONS

IS MOST RESPECTFULLY INSCRIBED.

CONTENTS.

SERMON XII.

PREPARATION FOR DEATH.

SERMON I.

THE CERTAINTY OF THE RESURRECTION[1].

St. John v. 28, 29.

" Marvel not at this: for the hour is coming, in the which all that are in the graves shall hear His voice, and shall come forth ; they that have done good, unto the resurrection of life ; and they that have done evil, unto the resurrection of damnation."

THE hour is coming ! The most wondrous event that is yet to come to pass in the future history of the world, whilst the most uncertain as regards the exact date of its occurrence, is yet certain of fulfilment. Distant and remote as it may be in the unknown and mysterious Future, still the hour is coming—is coming. It is nearer now, by the lapse of eighteen centuries, than when

[1] Preached at Westminster Abbey Special Services, Sunday evening, April 15, 1860.

B

the words of my text were first spoken. It
draws nearer and more near still with every
hour the passage of which is tolled with funeral
knell in our ears. It is nearer now than when
you entered within these walls this evening.
Inevitable Future! Setting in towards us as
the resistless tide from some distant shore; ever
flowing in a silent stream which cannot be
stayed! Yesterday we spoke of this day as To-
morrow. To-morrow we shall speak of it as
Yesterday. Gradually, insensibly, Future becomes Present, and Present recedes into Past,
as a mountain rivulet expands into the broader
river, and the river is merged and absorbed
in the vaster sea. So that hour will be as this
hour. It will pass from Future to Present.
It is coming! It is utterly impossible to forbid
that the next hour shall come. Even if this
world should cease to be, if this present system
should be blotted out of Creation, that which we
ordinarily speak of as Time would nevertheless
continue. For Time is no more than an arbitrary
division, a breaking up into smaller fragments of
the more grand and large conception of Eternity.
Years and months, days and hours, minutes and
seconds are helps to the finite understanding,
enabling it the better to realize that which is

another name and idea of God. So long as God exists there will be a Future. Hence there is a deep and awful significance in these words, "*the hour is coming.*"

It belongs to Omniscience so clearly to foresee as to speak of any event in the Future as if it were already Present. No veil of imperfection obscures the vision of God. All history is planned and pre-arranged in the mind and counsels of the Infinite Being. When our Saviour spake these words He in one sense prophesied, but they were the prediction of One to Whom all yet future was present. His eye ranged at a glance over all the years to come. Already He felt inwardly possessed of that life in Himself which was to quicken the dead into newness of spiritual life. He felt endued with that authority which is yet to be exercised in the sight of assembled worlds. In view of the coming day of His own exaltation He announced that on which Christianity hinges—"The hour is coming, in the which all that are in the graves shall hear His voice."

What is this event which is so certainly to come to pass, as certainly as that God exists, placed now as it is beyond all reasonable doubt or controversy, cleared of the misty speculation of heathen philosophy, leaving no longer any room for scepticism? What is that grand central truth without which our faith is vain, our hope of eternal life without foundation—all preaching but idle tales, this life present inexplicable, Christianity itself a fable, its Founder, apostles, and missionaries only successful impostors? What is this event looming in the far distant horizon, for which all creation, as with outstretched neck, is waiting with impatient longing, "the earnest expectation of the creature?" What is that which silences the cavil of the sceptic, when, from his narrow view of things, the prevalence of vice over virtue would lead him to doubt an overruling Providence, or the justice of the Most High God? What is that which Science forbids the Atheist to hold impossible, and which, if we well consider it, gives to this life present all its significance, reconciles its apparent inconsistencies, explains satisfactorily the permission of evil, accounts for the disharmony which everywhere prevails, and solves those enigmas which suggest themselves to every thoughtful mind? What is that which enhances every good action with a prospective value, which lends a dignity to Truth, Justice, Love, Purity, and, on the other hand, makes Sin so terrible and so dreadful to

contemplate in all its consequences? What is
that which you at once recognize as the great incentive to holiness, and the thought of which is
perhaps the only real check upon the headstrong
impulses of our fallen nature? Why should we
experience remorse or fear after the violation of
God's laws, when there is no immediate prospect of punishment, or even of exposure and
detection? What is the true meaning of those
self-reproaches when others do not so much as
suspect us of a fault? Why should the memory
and consciousness of a committed sin haunt and
harass the mind, years after the actual transgression, as some shadow that will not pass away?
There must be some meaning in all this—some
momentous truth involved and implied in it.

Or again, what is the lesson which Nature at
this season of the year so eloquently teaches us?
Why should the season itself be so especially
welcome to every mind open to the reception
of truth? What is that acceptable instruction
which Spring conveys, speaking in the language
of renewal and revival in this her Easter illustration of Christian verities? For they are not
new, but the same old truths which God would
impress on the mind of man, repeating and
reiterating them, that they may be more realized

and recognized by us. The everlasting hills speak of His sure and unchangeable promises; the vault of Heaven of His infinitude; the Ocean mirrors forth His eternity; the Earth, with its teeming and varied wonders, is eloquent of His power; Autumn, with its deciduous foliage, reminds us that we all do fade as a leaf. With each returning Spring God would teach us the same consoling truth. As often as it returns in the revolving seasons so often it reminds us, with all the charm of its associations, of the wondrous truth of Resurrection from the dead. See now the bursting leaf, the greenness of foliage, the fresh life breathed forth, as by the breath of the everlasting Spirit, into all the countless phases of sentient existence! See the quickening principle infused into all which long time had lain torpid and desolate in its wintry dreariness, and now, casting off her funeral garb, Nature is presented to us in that more pleasing aspect which belongs to the very idea of Easter.

The outer world confirms that which our finer instincts suggest, of which the soul itself is prophetic, which robs death of its sting, and the grave of its victory, which enables sorrowing relatives to commit to the earth the loved remains of kinsmen with words of cheerful expectation, which gives now to every grave and to every churchyard a hallowed tenantry of sacred dust, and makes it the jealous guardian of that which only awaits the sound of the Archangel's trumpet to reappear in sensible identity and reality of being. This is the truth on which all our belief is centred, and which is established beyond dispute by the Resurrection of Jesus Christ from the dead, —viz. the Resurrection of our bodies. "The hour is coming, in the which all that are in the graves shall hear His voice, and shall come forth; they that have done good, unto the resurrection of life; and they that have done evil, unto the resurrection of damnation."

The Resurrection of our bodies. This is a fact distinct from that of the Immortality of the soul. The faith of many stumbles at the former. Our whole spiritual being is an argument for the latter. It is difficult, nay impossible, to conceive that the immaterial element in man can ever perish. We have no reason whatever to believe that it is affected by decay, or by the general shock of death. On the contrary, the presumption is that the soul survives the dissolution of the body. The deepest thinkers in all ages have held the immortality of the soul to be at least highly probable, and this general belief has been expressed in various modes more or less correct, and in accordance with the popular creed, whether of mythology, superstition, or unadulterated truth. Most men have an instinctive belief in the immortality of the soul. Futurity and immortality are consistent even with Atheism. We are individually and separately conscious of the residence within ourselves of a something distinct from and unlike to our outward physical organism. It is this consciousness, indeed, which constitutes individuality. We possess a two-fold nature—the outward material form—"the inward" and immaterial, without any definite shape or figure. We see that the body is susceptible of growth and decay, increased by the assimilation to itself of substances which contribute to its gradual enlargement, liable to injury, the prey of a thousand ills, any one of which is of itself sufficient to bring about death. We know of no other causes of death than such as are matter of familiar experience, experiment, and observation. We have no reason to believe that the soul is affected by any one of these. On the contrary, we know that it is not. The knife of the surgeon as it cuts through the quivering flesh does not touch any portion of the thinking principle. According to well-known and estab-

lished facts, we have several times over lost a
great part, or perhaps the whole of our body,
yet·we remain the same living beings. And
though there are some bodily injuries, which
from the intimate and subtle nature of the connexion between mind and matter, impair the
mental faculties, still there are on record the
most convincing proofs that this is but a temporary disturbance and derangement. Even up
to the latest moment of human existence, though
the body be the prey of a wasting sickness,—the
strength so prostrate that the pulse of life is
scarcely perceptible, and all physical energy well
nigh spent,—the mind is not only unaffected,
but even then asserts its indestructibility by the
vigour it displays in the presence of death.
" Though the outward man perish, yet the inward man is renewed day by day[2]."

Hence, as you will doubtless have often observed, it was not so much *immortality* as the
resurrection, which Christ taught. That, for
which St. Paul contends in the Fifteenth Chapter
of the First Epistle to the Corinthians, and on
which all his arguments are brought to bear, is
not the doctrine of a future life, but distinctly
this of the resurrection of the flesh, " not of a

[2] 2 Cor. iv. 16.

formless existence hereafter, but of a future existence in a form." As yet, this had not been distinctly revealed. We recognize the germs of truth in the deification of all that was good and noble amongst the Greeks. The Pythagorean doctrine of the transmigration of souls, according to which the spirits of the departed were invested with other bodies, suited to the disposition and capacities they manifested in this present life, was, at least, more philosophical than that which would limit such an association of soul and body to this present life only. The resurrection of the body as it was not distinctly revealed prior to the coming of Christ, so it is at once the great historical proof of the truth of Christianity. It is that cardinal doctrine which St. Paul seemed to impersonate when he preached to the Athenians, " Jesus and the Resurrection." Christ, as the representative of our humanity, took upon Himself that humanity in its fullest signification. It was our human nature which He assumed when He was born of the Virgin. It was our human nature in which He hungered and suffered. It was our human nature in which He died in agony on the Cross. It was our human nature which was laid with Him in the sepulchre. It was our human nature which Thomas

saw and handled, after our Lord had risen from
the grave. By virtue of our union with Him,
and by virtue of His resurrection, we are assured
indubitably of our own. There is henceforth
an indissoluble association established. Whether
we believe or disbelieve, the fact of Christ having
identified Himself physically with humanity, and
of the intimate union of the human with the
divine, has brought about this, as a necessary
consequence, that there belongs now to every
human being a nature redeemed everlastingly
from the grave. We are possessed of a nature
over which Death has no annihilating power, no
perpetual dominion ; a nature which so bears
upon it the stamp and superscription of Divinity,
that though it sleep for centuries in the sleep
of oblivion, though it undergo the process of
corruption, and become so completely disintegrated that scarce any visible trace of it shall
be left, still " the hour is coming,"—the hour
is coming when the power of Christ's resurrection shall make itself felt, and be triumphantly
exercised over it. It is no longer a matter on
which we may entertain a doubt. Observe not
only the certainty, but the universality of this
great truth—" *all* that are in the graves shall
hear His voice."

Herein, moreover, lies the essential difference between the immortality of heathen philosophy, and the immortality of the Christian's creed. Apart from the resurrection of the body the Bible holds out, perhaps, not one distinct hope of the immortality of the soul. For all we know the soul may be capable of high bliss dissociated from the body, and Omnipotence might provide for it some sphere suitable to its ethereal nature, but not to insist on the difficulty of conceiving a state of sentient enjoyment apart from, and independent of some physical organism, we know that redemption were incomplete, and nothing less than a signal failure, if the body were left to moulder in the grave, and were not to be re-united to that which had once tabernacled in it. Scripture nowhere sanctions that idea in current phraseology, which would have us believe that the body is no more than an incubus on the mind, and that hereafter no material organization shall compass or enrobe the immortal spirit. True, indeed, that now the body is the instrument of sin. Through its several senses, as through so many avenues and open doors, solicitations and temptations from without approach us. The earnest-minded amongst you often say with St. Paul, " Who shall deliver me

from the body of this death?" You would fain
imagine that a severance for ever from so burden-
some an alliance would at once ensure you freedom
from all occasions of sin. But no! the body
must yet be redeemed. As the spiritual part of
man may be purified, so the material and physical
may be glorified and made a nobler thing. As
far as we know, the uniform tendency of all
physical research represents the body as the indispensable organ of the mind for action, if not
for thought. Indeed we cannot form any distinct
and intelligible notion of the separate existence
of the soul. Christianity directs our most eager
expectations, not to the emancipation of the soul
from that which is commonly called its "prison,"
but rather to the final redemption of this our
outward form. "Not that we would be unclothed, but clothed upon, that mortality may be
swallowed up of life."

And, therefore, it is, that in the hour of our
bitter sorrow we can look with calmer confidence
upon the pallid and wasted features of one from
whom the spirit is departed, and who has passed
on before us into the unseen world, leaving us for
a while in sadness and in tears. Heartrending
as is the separation from those whom we dearly
love in life, how much more so would it be if we

knew and felt that we were looking for the very last time upon that countenance, endeared to memory by a thousand ties of endearment; that the eye which had so often returned our look with fond expression, was closed for ever in death; that the touch of the vanished hand should never again be felt; that the voice once so full of tenderness was for ever and for ever silenced in the unbroken stillness of the entombing sepulchre! How much greater would be our grief if we thought we were consigning to the grave of annihilation, to be henceforth utterly effaced from the record of creation, the lifeless remains of our parent, husband, wife, child, or friend, with whose life ours had been so closely linked and interwoven! No, this cannot be. Our whole nature declares against so hopeless a doom. The mourners are met at the churchyard entrance with words from our Burial Service expressive of a truth in accordance with our innermost convictions. As the body is lowered down into the grave, we feel that even in death there is infused into that lifeless corpse, as so much leaven, the mysterious secret of its vitality; that it contains within itself the hidden germ of future life. We leave it resting there, it may be for long and many years, still, we leave it in confident, hopeful expectation of reunion. Every grain, every atom of its hallowed dust is in the guardianship of a faithful Creator. So that the language of our Burial Service falls as some softer strain of music on the ear of mourners. " I am the Resurrection and the Life, saith the Lord : he that believeth in Me, though he were dead, yet shall he live : and whosoever liveth and believeth in Me shall never die³." Again, " It is sown in corruption ; it is raised in incorruption. It is sown in dishonour ; it is raised in glory. It is sown in weakness ; it is raised in power. It is sown a natural body ; it is raised a spiritual body⁴."

Great indeed is this mystery. Who, as he passes through a churchyard, and sees around him the sealed graves and the heavy tombstones, has not felt the doctrine of the Resurrection to be a wonderful mystery ? To the outward eye there is no sign of the nearness of this event. Men disappear from the midst of us, one by one, as autumn leaves fall from the tree. Life in its varied phases is always before the eye. The dead are quickly buried out of sight. But for the occasional circumstance which recalls them

---

³ John xi. 25, 26.   ⁴ 1 Cor. xv. 42, 43.

to our memory by the relic they bequeathed us;
but for the influence which they may have
exercised on the world, and left written in indelible characters on the face of society; but for
the monument which serves to indicate their
narrow resting-place, it is with them, and will
be with us, as if we had never been. The gap
we for a moment make is soon filled up. Generation succeeds generation, as wave breaks upon
wave, leaving no trace behind, save, perhaps,
some few fragments of seaweed cast upon the
seashore. Time does its silent work even upon
our tombstones, obliterating the letters which
the chisel has engraven upon them. Look
around you on these monuments grown grey
with old age. The stones beneath your feet
cover the remains of men who have figured in
this world's history. See how they are worn
away by the passing to and fro of the living.
This noble edifice in which we are assembled is
one vast shrine of the departed. Its walls are
eloquent of all that was most excellent in character, lofty in genius, distinguished for at-
tainments, splendid in position, illustrious in
birth and station. We are here, the living
amongst the dead. The scene of our worship
here this evening is consecrated to our minds by

the thought of all the great, and good, and noble,
whose remains are entombed here. If we could
remove these grave-stones, if we could look
down into the dark and yawning vaults beneath
them, in how many would scarce so much as a
trace be discovered of that which was the theme of
poet's praise, of the sculptor's chisel, of a nation's
pride! You ask, Is there indeed a Resurrection? Will all these, who have in years
past been laid here, rise again? With what
body shall they come? We know that that
which is buried in the grave moulders away
into kindred dust. No fact is better established
than that of the Circulation of Matter. Che-
mical science, physiological research establish
beyond all dispute that the human body is
composed of substances which by constant assimilation contribute to its growth, and which as
soon as life is extinct, are restored to the sources
whence they have been derived. In process of
time this our frame is resolved into the original
elements of its construction, passes into new
and other forms, is scattered and dissipated to
the four winds of heaven. Piece by piece, grain
by grain, atom by atom, it becomes so completely disintegrated that you shall search in
vain for any traces of it. Thus in the lapse

of centuries the earth throughout its length and breadth becomes one vast receptacle of immortal seed. "All that tread the globe are but a handful to the tribes that slumber in its bosom."

> *" Tell me, thou dust beneath my feet,*
> *Thou dust that once hadst breath,*
> *Tell me how many mortals meet*
> *In this small hill of death ?"*

The earth is broadcast and thickly sown with the germs of the future and spiritual harvest. Like seed cast into the ground, it must die that it may bring forth fruit. It awaits but the quickening power and voice which shall give and call it into new existence.

Mysterious as it is, and beyond our finite comprehension, yet we dare not doubt that this shall be. Who shall limit the creative power of God? Say not within thine heart that He Who created worlds where worlds were not, Who has studded Space with countless planets, Who has peopled the Universe with innumerable forms, has so exhausted His creative power that He cannot provide for the glorified spirit and for the soul redeemed a form suited to enshrine and embody it. The Resurrection of Christ is synony-

mous with our own. Science positively declares
that no particle of matter is ever lost. The same
Being who created us out of the dust can recreate
us at His sovereign will. We cannot tell how
all these scattered elements shall be so regathered
as that we shall be reinvested with that identity
by which we were known and recognized amongst
our fellow-men. Yet the resurrection will not be
a greater wonder than was the work of the first
creation. Omnipotence holds in Its grasp every
atom which floats upon the sunbeam. There is
nothing lost or annihilated in the Universe of
God. Nothing is so scattered or dissipated that
His voice cannot reach it and bid it imperatively
to obey His summons. He who foresaw all things
foresaw also this. When all is mature and ripe for
the harvest the sound of the Archangel's trump
shall break over every sepulchre and penetrate
with awakening echoes into every tomb. Life
shall be communicated to every atom now sleeping in the dust, and from countless graves there
shall start forth into renewed existence the buried
generations of the past. The sea shall give up
her dead from fathomless depths. The earth
shall heave to and fro with mighty birth-throes.
The voice, which called Lazarus forth, shall summon myriads upon myriads together, and not so

much as one shall be left behind in that last universal Easter.

Imagination in vain endeavours to realize this awful event. It will be, as if at this moment there were heard suddenly amongst us the pealing of the trumpet-sound resounding and resounding with startling echoes throughout this cathedral, and some unearthly voice should bid the spirits of the departed return from the shadowy land into which they have passed, and rushing into their renewed tabernacles, obedient to its commands, the dead should come forth from beneath our feet and reappear in living reality and identity of being.

Imagine this. Imagine not one left in his grave. Picture to your mind's eye that which is but a very imperfect, a very limited conception of the resurrection of all creation; a poor illustration of that stupendous event thus predicted and yet to be fulfilled.

"The hour is coming, in the which all that are in the graves shall hear His voice, and shall come forth; they that have done good, unto the resurrection of life; and they that have done evil, unto the resurrection of damnation."

My brethren, as believers in the great truths of Revelation, suffer me now to speak to you with all the solemnity and earnestness which this subject suggests. Let me speak to you as to immortal beings, as to men who are in earnest about their salvation. There is no one of us here present who may dismiss the subject from his mind with indifference, because there is no one of us who can escape immortality. We *must* rise from the dead. If there be no such thing as annihilation known in the Universe, if the soul within us be immaterial and imperishable, if the word of God be true, if the Resurrection of Christ be a fact which infidelity cannot gainsay or deny, then our resurrection also is sure. Difficult as the subject may be, the difficulties of Atheism are still greater. The Resurrection of Christ, and the resurrection of all men are so indissolubly connected, that you prove or disprove both, in proving or disproving either. See you not what deep and significant meaning, viewed in connexion with this subject, such expressions as these possess : of our being *"one with Christ,"* of being *"united with Him," "buried with Christ in His death," "risen with Christ ?"* Is it not of all importance that we believe in Him in whom all our eternal interests are centred ? Better, better far, that we should never stir from the grave in which men have laid us, that the scattered elements should refuse to be reunited, were that possible, than that we should close our eyes in death, without this mysterious union with our risen Lord Himself having been first established.   Better, better far, that we sleep the sleep of an oblivion that knows no waking, than rise from our graves to have no part in the resurrection of the just.

What real influence for good does this truth exercise over us habitually ?   Is it ever present to our minds, sobering our thoughts, quickening our energies, filling us with holy and salutary fear ?   Do you realize in all its personal, individual relation, the certainty of your own resurrection ; that you, your very self, must rise from the dead ; that in the consciousness of your own individuality, you must one day stand in the immediate, actual, living presence of the Judge of the whole earth, and see Him face to face ?   As year after year in its rapid passage brings us inevitably so much nearer to the day of His appearing, are we becoming more and more prepared for it ?   Do you believe in Jesus Christ, earnestly desiring to be possessed of Him—to be united with Him by a living and lively faith, and to be already quickened by that life by which He quickeneth whom He will ?

Are you being sensibly renewed day by day by the sanctifying, regenerating influence of the Spirit of God, so that Christ is being formed in you? Are you striving, through the mighty aid of that Spirit, to overcome the soul-destroying lusts, the sinful passions, the evil tempers of your fallen nature? Do you pray frequently, not only for temporal mercies, but chiefly, and before all other requests, for all those higher spiritual gifts and graces which self-examination on your knees has taught you to pray for, and which, as we possess them, make us meet for the inheritance of the saints in light? Look at this assembled congregation, representing various shades and differences of character. There is nothing by which we may outwardly distinguish the evil from the good. It shall not always be so. The time draws nigh when a sharp and bold line of distinction will be drawn. "They that have done good; they that have done evil." Ask yourself, to what resurrection shall I rise? What is my daily life? The answer may be found in that. For is not this plainly to be gathered and inferred from this passage of Scripture, that Character survives the grave? The Present determines the Future. As the tree falls so it shall lie. By a necessary law we shall reap that which we have sown. What we shall be hereafter depends on what we are now. Every word, every action—it may be every thought,— tells upon eternity. These go before us to meet us there. I do not here speak of the means and opportunities we individually possess of doing good. I speak of the reference which all that we do and say has to the future. Our words cannot be unspoken, our deeds, good or evil, cannot be undone. Each day, each hour that we live, unseen influences, good and evil, surround us, and insensibly the character is being formed for its future destiny of bliss or woe. The besetting sin, whatever that may be, which clings to us from childhood upward, through manhood and womanhood, even to grey hairs, if it be not mastered and overcome, will rise up in judgment against us. So on the other hand, the life of holiness carries with it its sure and proper reward. Every act of devotion and of self-denial, every thwarting of our own will, every successful strife with old and sinful habits, every temptation resisted deepens our piety, and brings us nearer God. To you, who are endeavouring thus to live, and who are treading in the footsteps of our blessed Lord, the prospect of a resurrection should be the greatest stimulus to your piety.

Persevere in this Christian life. Persevere in it in the face of all the difficulties of the Christian life. Perseverance is essential to success. The Spirit in your heart is an earnest of your inheritance, of your union with Christ. Pray without ceasing for larger gifts of the Holy Ghost. Be not weary in well doing. Think much and often of the end of life; so you will be the better prepared for it when your summons comes. Set your affections now on things above. Live near to God. Thus your life will be blessed, and your end peaceful. You will fear no evil as the shadow of death is falling upon you, and you stand on the brink of its cold river.

Happy he who lives as he would die. Happy he who has so lived, that when his last hour is at hand, and he is about to pass hence into the unseen world, can comfort the mourners as they stand around him with words such as these, expressive of a simple, yet undoubting faith.

" It doth not yet appear what we shall be; but we know that, when He shall appear, we shall be like Him; for we shall see Him as He is[s]."

---

[s] 1 John iii. 2.

SERMON II.

Eph. iv. 30.

*" Grieve not the Holy Spirit of God, whereby ye
are sealed unto the day of redemption."*

My brethren, in commemorating, as we do
this day, the fulfilment of our Saviour's promise
to His disciples in the visible descent on the day
of Pentecost of the Holy Ghost, we are brought
face to face with another of those truths connected with our religious belief, which is confessedly mysterious and incomprehensible to our
finite understanding. The very name and appel-
lation assigned to the Third Person of the ever-
blessed Trinity, the word " Ghost," (the Saxon
Gast, or Spirit,) involves an idea which at once
removes the subject beyond the province of
human investigation. We can form, at best,

but a most vague and crude conception of the nature of Spirit. All that meets the eye in this material world around us, is embodied in some outward form which properly belongs to it. Every sound which strikes upon the ear is the result of certain vibrations, of wave-like impulses proceeding from a definite physical cause. The body is the highly complicated organ of sense, by which we are immediately brought into sensible contact with this external system. We cannot distinctly conceive the separate, independent existence of Spirit, still less its mode of operation, its form or other characteristic conditions of being. We have never seen a Spirit with our own eyes. All illustrations and metaphors necessarily fail to convey to the mind an adequate and intelligible idea of that which is supernatural and superhuman. The ordinary and vulgar idea of a ghost is rightly counted amongst the most fond of superstitious notions. The apparitions which have scared those who aver that they have seen them in the churchyard, amid the grouping shadows ,of twilight, in the solemn midnight hour, or under other favourable circumstances, have either been wanting in sufficient testimony to entitle them to credit, or on more sober examination have been proved to have been no more than the phantoms of the brain, creations of a disordered mind, the result of disease or ill-health, deranging the vision, and in many ways infecting the judgment. As a rule, ghost stories are listened to with more or less incredulity, and not without impatience, as idle tales with which to terrify unreflecting childhood into obedience, or to excite a morbid mind, greedy of the marvellous. They are unworthy of serious consideration. In discrediting however, these so-called and fanciful apparitions, we do not deny the existence of spirits, nor the fact of a spirit world. We only discredit the supposed apparition on the grounds that a spirit dissociated from the body, and made visible to mortal eye in mortal form, is that of which we have no conclusive evidence, which is wanting in sufficient proof to outweigh all the probabilities against any thing so inconsistent with this present system of things, and at variance with the common experience of mankind. That a world of spiritual beings does somewhere exist, though not capable of positive ocular demonstration, is nevertheless a revealed truth. The creative power of God is not to be limited to this or that particular form which we may happen to see. What is more striking than the almost unlimited variety to be observed in even that portion of

creation of which we are cognizant? And how
small is this our planet, compared with the
universe! Doubtless, man is only one of many
types of created beings. The exhaustless power
of God knows no such limitation as we, with our
finite knowledge, would arbitrarily impose.

The two-fold nature of man himself confirms
the revealed truth respecting the existence of
spirits. Every man has that within himself,
essential to his individuality, which he is conscious is of a nature wholly unlike his physical,
material organization. He possesses that which
he believes to be imperishable, immaterial, immortal, unaffected by decay or death, which no
rude hand can touch or destroy. Granted, as
Science seems more and more to establish, that
all the organic functions, and the conditions of
our outward life, depend on the continued presence and supply of food, air, light, heat, elec-
tricity; still there is an integral part of man, independent of these so-called Vital Forces, which
is not originated, sustained, nor affected by them.
That by which we individually reflect and reason,
by which we think and feel, that which is commonly called the soul, wherever it may reside in
the body, is that by which we are brought into
contact and communion with the world of spirits,

with that unseen world which lies all around us, and in which we believe. Hence, in the idea of the existence of the Holy Ghost, there is nothing *primâ facie* improbable, nothing contrary to reason; rather it is in harmony with the spiritual element in man upon which He directly acts. We cannot, indeed, describe Him as He really is, because we have nothing with which we may compare Him. At best we must speak of Him in language metaphorical, and illustrated by familiar objects. We have no correct idea of His nature and essence, therefore we can have no proper words in which to express it, because words are no more than the signs of ideas. The terms employed in speaking of the Holy Ghost are such as most fitly express His nature, so far as we can comprehend it. In the Creed, while we say that Christ was *begotten* of the Father, implying *generation*, we affirm of the Holy Ghost that He is neither made nor created, nor begotten, but *proceeding*. Again, in the Nicene Creed we say, "I believe in the Holy Ghost, the Lord and Giver of Life, Who *proceedeth* from the Father and the Son." In keeping with this idea of a spiritual influence is the express language of St. John when he describes our Lord's appearance to His disciples on the evening of the first day of the week after His resurrection. " He *breathed* on them, and saith unto them, Receive ye the Holy Ghost[1]." When He assumed an outward visible form, it was that of cloven tongues like as of fire, which sat upon each of the assembled apostles[2]. At other times His presence was attested by the shaking of the place where they were assembled[3].

If we cannot describe the *nature* of the Holy Ghost, still less can we define the *mode* of His mysterious operations on the human mind. We are not able to discern His motions. We cannot trace the path by which, in answer to some earnest prayer, He descends from Heaven, nor detect His viewless, yet sanctifying and ener- gizing agency in the hearts of individual men. Sometimes He is there, so plainly, so evidently, so unmistakeably, that we say of one who is under His blessed influence, as Pharaoh said of Joseph, " *Can we find such a one as this is, a man in whom the Spirit of God is*[4] *?* " as the Evan- gelist records of our blessed Saviour, " *Jesus, being full of the Holy Ghost, returned from Jordan*[5] *;* " as St. Peter of those Gentile con-

---

[1] John xx. 22.   [2] Acts ii. 3.
[3] Acts iv. 31.   [4] Gen. xli. 31.
[5] Luke iv. 1.

verts, who spake with tongues and magnified
God, " *Can any man forbid water, that these
should not be baptized, which have received the
Holy Ghost as well as we* [6] *?* " At other times
the absence or withdrawal of the Spirit of God
is as marked, as in the case of Elymas the
sorcerer, whom St. Paul thus rebuked, " O full
of all subtlety and all mischief, thou child of the
devil, thou enemy of all righteousness, wilt thou
not cease to pervert the right ways of the
Lord [7]?"

Although the descent and operations of the
Spirit be not visually discernible, though it be
itself "as the wind which bloweth where it
listeth, and thou hearest the sound thereof, but
canst not tell whence it cometh, nor whither it
goeth," mysterious as this confessedly is, it is not
unlike other facts with which we are familiar.
The natural philosopher is continually being
brought face to face with those ultimate laws or
facts of which his discoveries are only so many
phases or developments, brought to light by experiment and research. The various phenomena
of nature are simply the varied results of the
operation of nature's ultimate laws. The philo-

---

[6] Acts x. 47.   [7] Acts xiii. 10.

sopher sees no more than these results. He cannot account for what he witnesses in the laboratory, or observes in the great system around us,
beyond a certain, recognized, and limited point?
He refers all these developments, all these discoveries, to that ultimate law of gravitation or
affinity to which they properly belong. Beyond
this he cannot push his inquiries. He accepts
that law, and is content to observe its conditions
and its operations. Limited as is the point of
view in which he may see it, it is sufficiently intelligible and clear to satisfy his mind of its existence, and for all the practical purposes of life.

. Not otherwise is it in the spiritual world. The
existence of the Holy Ghost as a distinct Person
in the undivided Trinity, His presence in the
world, is known only by the effects produced.
With this we must rest content. It is all that
we really require to know. All that is good in
this fallen world we refer to Him, as the Source
of all good. We recognize His agency in the en-
lightenment of the world. We discern His presence in the changed, renewed, converted soul.
He is seen in one, the whole tenour of whose life
and conversation presents a marked contrast to
that of the worldly and unspiritually-minded.
We recognize Him in the restraining influence

D

He exercises over one man, while the unruly will of another as surely betrays the want of such a salutary restraint over the passions and affections of our fallen nature. Great is the work assigned to the Holy Ghost, varied are His offices. All that is lovely and harmonious in Nature is the work of the Spirit. He brooded over the infant world in its rude, chaotic state, and out of the confusion and disharmony which every where prevailed, He shaped the finished work of the glorious Universe. When the eye surveys with delight some far-spreading landscape of varied beauty, verdant meadow, silvery stream, wooded copse, azure sky ever changing in its aspect with shifting light and shade, as now the sunbeam illumines the scene, or shadows chase one another over the plain, there comes this elevating thought to the mind, over and above the gratification such scenery brings to the outward sense, that all this charm of landscape, this inexpressible and exquisite beauty, is due to the transforming agency of the Spirit of God. Alike in her wild and rugged mountain scenes, by the shore of the sleeping sea, under the star-lit canopy of heaven, and amidst her softer beauties, Nature testifies to the handiwork of the Spirit, creation

bears the impress of Deity, the Universe reflects
in its harmony and order the mind of God. And
that which He is to the material, physical world,
reducing to order the chaotic confusion of air and
earth and water, He is to the moral and spiritual
world also. The special office of the Holy Ghost
is to regenerate the soul of man, as He renewed
the material Universe in which He dwells.
That is His distinct work and office. He is
sent and given that He may effect in each one
of us that new birth without which no man
can enter into the Kingdom of God—that
new birth—that great inward spiritual change,
which no one can mistake who has under-
gone and experienced it—that passing from
death unto life, unintelligible to him who is
yet lying in darkness and in the shadow of
death.

This wondrous change, which we ordinarily
speak of as *conversion*, scarcely admits of verbal
definition. It is more a matter of *feeling* than
of *words*, yet not of suddenly-excited, spasmodic
impulse, but of calm, settled, sober resolution and
purpose. Nor, again, is this moral change
effected violently, all at once, but most commonly in a manner analogous to all great changes.
It is gradual, like the unfolding of the leaf, or

the expanding of the bud into the flower, under
the genial influences of Spring. As it has been
well observed, " Rude and sudden changes usually
mark the works of man. It is not so with the
works of Nature, which generally increase by
gradual and scarcely perceptible transitions,
which require the lapse of some time to make
.them in any degree remarkable." The mission
of the Holy Ghost is to infuse into the world at
large, and into individual men, spiritual energy
and life. Wherever the Gospel of Christ is proclaimed, the Spirit accompanies the message of
salvation. He interprets Scripture to the untutored mind of the heathen—to the mean understanding of the unlearned. He is here in
this House of God. There is not one of us
assembled here who has not been, at some period
or other, the subject of His operation and influence. For consider what are some of the
effects and operations of the Holy Ghost. He
illumines the mind and understanding, making
that clear which before had been dark and unmeaning. He enables us more firmly to believe,
for faith is of the Spirit of God. He comforts
under the world's sorrows or anxieties. He testifies of Christ. He assures us of our adoption as
sons of God in Christ Jesus. By Him we are

joined to Christ, "being all baptized by one Spirit into one body." He is the appointed guide through the mazy paths of life, leading us into all truth, quickening the conscience and making it more sensitive, enabling our fallible and erring minds to form a right judgment in all things. He warns us by some unearthly voice addressed to our inmost soul, when temptation is at hand, or when our sinful passions would lead us into wilful sin. He upholds by His sustaining presence those who desire, amid failures and shortcomings and imperfect acts, to please God. He seals us with some mark of His own. He sets a stamp of recognition on the very dust of our mouldering remains—an indelible, indestructible mark "by which the Lord knoweth them that are His," and by which when the morning of the Resurrection-day breaks in the Eastern heavens, every sincere, believing Christian shall have secured to him that inheritance of which the Spirit is at once the earnest and the pledge.

No less, my brethren, no less than this is the mission, the work of the Spirit. What we want is to realize more fully than we do the ever-active agency, the personal presence, the working of the self-same Spirit as really *now* as in

the bygone days of His more open manifestations.   Though we do not witness an actual
visible descent of the Holy Ghost, nor any
miraculous proofs of His presence, we have
abundant testimony of His continued agency
as seen in His *ordinary* workings, gifts, and
graces; yet how few of us realize and bring
home to ourselves the personality and presence of
the Holy Spirit!   How few of us habitually live
in the consciousness that we are at all times
within the sphere of a Divine Person—loving,
compassionate—Who from our childhood, through
all our years has been striving with us, guiding
us, bearing with us!   And yet we shall never
pray for the Spirit aright, nor, indeed, think of
Him aright, nor reverence Him as deeply as we
should, unless we do thus realize Him—unless
we habituate our minds to the awful and solemn
thought, that God the Holy Ghost is ever near
us, ever about our path, not as a mere influence,
divine afflatus, energy, or some equally vague
idea, but in that strictly personal sense which
Scripture in this and many similar passages
emphatically sets forth.   " Grieve not the Holy
Spirit of God, whereby ye are sealed unto the
day of redemption."

     " Grieve not the Holy Spirit of God!"   Grieve

not! So solemn a warning as this enables us
also to apply a searching test. We may examine
ourselves, that our spiritual experience may supply additional testimony to the personality of
the Holy Ghost. " Grieve not the Holy Spirit
of God." Probably there is nothing which, consciously and wilfully, or unconsciously and in
ignorance, we more often do than this. Most of
us, if not all, can readily recall to mind those
bitter feelings of remorse which we have experienced after the commission of some sin, or
when we have yielded to the force of temptation,
or been betrayed into the suddenly excited evil
temper, or spoken hasty and uncharitable words.
Sometimes, on trying occasions, our moral
courage has been put to the test, and we have
been traitors to the cause of Christ. You know
yourself how poignant have been your after-re-
grets, how bitter your self-reproaches, when, the
force of passion spent, or the exciting occasion
passed, you have returned to yourself and have
felt that you had grieved the Spirit of God. For
it is a solemn thought that we may resist the
grace of God, we may quench the Spirit. He is
not so irresistible in His operations that we may
not counteract them, neutralize their efficacy,
defeat their object. Even where that blessed work

is begun in our hearts, its completion is not of
course or of necessity. No. By little and by
little, at first heedlessly and thoughtlessly, then
by every kind of compromise and excuse, at last,
by deliberate efforts of the will, that gentle
voice is hushed and stilled and quieted into a
fatal silence. All the better impulses that He
has inspired are checked—the holier aspirations
to which He has given birth are stifled in their
growth—the fire He has enkindled on the altar
of our hearts is damped and extinguished.
Little by little, by not heeding His dictates, by
steeling our hearts against Him, by opposing
Him, by deliberate and habitual disregard of the
Spirit of God—given us in our infancy at the
Font in answer to earnest prayers, given us
at our Confirmation—of which we have once
tasted,—grieved, despised, failing in His efforts,
He is withheld, and is withdrawn as if He had
never been given! Then a moral and spiritual
darkness sets in, a darkness as when in broad
noon-day light the sun in the heavens is eclipsed.
We are given over to a reprobate mind, given
over as a ship which has lost her rudder in the
fury of the gale, and the leak has sprung, and,
deserted by her crew, she is abandoned to the re-
lentless waves, driven hither and thither the

sport of wind and water, stranded at last in her helplessness on the bleak and inhospitable shore, or foundering in the fathomless depths of the engulfing seas. This is the history of the declension of many, and of many who once promised well; this the secret of their degeneracy, this the cause of their sad and mournful spiritual ruin. Too often have they grieved the Spirit of God, and at last He has departed from them !

Who is there here who has never been conscious of the strivings of the Holy Spirit? Who has not known those moments of more than usual solemnity, of unwonted impressiveness, when he thought seriously, when serious reflections on death, judgment, eternity were almost forced upon him?

When you were lying on the bed of sickness, lying there alone, with stillness all around, not a disturbing sound to be heard, uncertain what turn that sickness might take, has not the Spirit striven with you, when your mind was disquieted and full of fear, when you knew not but that that sickness might prove your last and fatal?

Standing by the bedside of one dear to you, watching the feeble flame of life flickering, now dying down, now reviving, at last going out in darkness, on such an occasion as this has not the Spirit of God striven with some who are here, survivors of an impressive death-bed scene? In the hour of bereavement and grief, when widowhood or orphanhood was new, and the wound of sorrow still fresh and bleeding, has not that same Spirit drawn near, and pleaded and striven?

As the hands of Christ's minister rested on your bowed head, and the soft strains of sacred music floated around you, and the prayer was being offered up that you might daily increase in God's Holy Spirit more and more, did you not at your Confirmation feel that that Spirit was verily near you?

When some words, casually spoken in the course of the sermon to which you were listening, went home to your conscience as words never went before, penetrating as a sword, piercing up to the very hilt, so applicable, so pointed, that you thought the preacher must know your circumstances, your besetting sin, your spiritual state, was not the Spirit manifesting then His power? Was not that clearly His voice carrying conviction to your mind, riveting those words on your attention?

So in many and various ways, have you not

known occasional better impulses, holier desires? Has not something followed you every where, into the secrecy of retirement, into the gay circles of society and fashionable life, gone with you, haunting you as some phantom, from which no darkness could screen you, yet no light discover to you, appealing to your better nature, elevating, even momentarily, your mind—waiting and waiting still—watching for some favouring moment and opportunity when He might gain entrance and admission into the soul?

> *" His is that gentle voice you hear,*
> *Soft as the breath of even,*
> *Which checks each thought, which calms each*
> *fear,*
> *And speaks of Heaven."*

And how have you met these advances? How have you received the Spirit when thus He has striven with you? Has the dangerous illness been a season of real spiritual blessing? Have you risen from your bed an altered man, or, with restored health, have all those serious reflections given place, one by one, to those less salutary which come too often with returning elasticity of spirits, with conscious safety and renewed

vigour of life? Has the voice which spoke
to you in the hour of sorrow, and which would
have you interpret that bereavement as a token
of love from Him "who doth not willingly
afflict the children of men," has that voice
gradually faded away into silence, as soon as
the first gush of anguish was over, and the mind
recovered its wonted cheerfulness through the
dissipating influence of Time? How long—
how long has that serious impression been retained which was yours as you stood by the
bedside of the dying, as you fondly gazed
for the last time, with awe and sadness, on
the placid features of your departed friend?
Have you allowed yourself to be guided and
directed by that Divine Guide Whose presence
was implored at your Confirmation; or ever
since that day have you only more and more
relapsed from even that degree of the Christian
life? When those words were spoken which
so struck and riveted your attention, have you
gone, on your return to your home, into your
own room, and while the impression was still
fresh and vivid, have you knelt down in silence,
and pondered on your knees over what you
have heard, and prayed God for Christ's sake
to bless your soul with the gift of His Spirit,

to perfect the good work thus begun? Or have you allowed some trifling conversation with the first friend you meet as you leave the House of God to displace that serious impression, and to distract your mind by other and more congenial topics? Are all our better impulses leading us to something further? Do they really influence us for good? Do we desire something more lasting than mere *lively feeling*, something more permanent than transient and fleeting *impression?* Oh! how often are these impulses, these feelings, these impressions discouraged, lest they should lead us further than we can yet make up our minds to go; discouraged through very fear of following the leadings of God's Spirit! We hesitate to receive the Holy Communion, because we feel that to receive it worthily we must change the whole course and complexion of our life; some cherished sin must be abandoned, some lust crucified, some sinful habit overcome; we must go less into society, must mix less in the scenes of fashion, must do less as the world around us does, must live a more consistent, holy life, a life more separate from the world, and nearer to God. How often something has seemed to say, as we were preparing to leave the House

in which the fair white linen cloth has been
spread before our eyes, "Shut not out yourself
from the blessings which wait on Christ's Ordinance. Why are you not purposing to remain
with the rest? Why habitually, and again
to-day, do you turn your back on the Lord's
Table?" In not believing that voice, in shutting
our ears against that remonstrance, we have
again and again "grieved the Spirit."

When some hard choice has to be made between
pleasure and duty, between our own inclinations
and the supreme Will of God, are the motions
of conscience—admonitions as these are of God—
are they obeyed? When we are about to enter
some scene, which we know beforehand will be
full of danger to our soul's health, is that Spirit,
Who meets us at the very threshold, and with
mild, constraining voice, beseeches us to keep at
the greatest possible distance from sin,—is He
obeyed? Do we grieve the Spirit by neglected
prayer—by frequent, deliberate acts of sin—
by want of charity—by an unholy temper?
Do we grieve Him by those more refined and
subtle faults and sins, such as pride, selfishness,
fastidious refinement, supercilious confidence in
self? Do we stifle the spiritual life by empty,
unworthy, frivolous trifling; by ease, luxury,

and sloth; by softness, self-indulgence, and too ready acquiescence in relaxed maxims of the world?

It is not too much, my Christian brethren, to say that we are lost or saved for ever, as we individually resist God's grace, or yield up ourselves to His sovereign power. What though we do not actually, visibly, by outward sense see the Holy Ghost? We have all in some measure felt His presence. Who of us would not be holier, more advanced in the knowledge of Christ, had we only more often heeded and obeyed the Spirit? Who must not attribute his or her present deadness, and coldness, and unspirituality of mind simply to the absence, to the withdrawing of God's Spirit? We cannot be too faithful, we cannot be too earnest with men in this matter. What is your own spiritual state? What is your own experience? Have you the Spirit of God? Have you once known His presence, once tasted of the Holy Ghost, and do you feel that He is now withheld or withdrawn? Does He now guide you? Does He sensibly, consciously influence you, not fitfully, and only occasionally, but *always*, all the day long, so that your daily walk and conversation is such as becometh the Gospel of Christ? Do you pray for the gift of the Holy Ghost, constantly, importunately, earnestly, praying for that high gift before all other requests? Do you every morning, ere you enter on the known duties and unknown trials of each new day, ask God for the sake of Christ, and for the sake of your own immortal soul, that He would not withhold His Spirit, but that He would give It you to strengthen you in the performance of every duty, to forearm you against every temptation or trial? Do you ask for It not carelessly, or with indifference to the result of your prayer, but anxiously waiting for and expecting the reply, because you are inwardly persuaded that "if any man have not the Spirit of Christ, he is none of His?"

Oh! seek that Spirit, my brethren. Seek Him each one for himself and for herself, on this, the anniversary day of Pentecost. Consider each of us what most we need, whether it be a more clear apprehension of divine truth, or an increase of faith, or peace of mind under life's anxieties, or comfort under some secret sorrow, or a greater knowledge of Christ, a more vivid, believing trust in His all-sufficiency, a deeper sense of our sinfulness, and of His infinite, atoning love. Seek Him for your safeguard, who, young and inexperienced, have life still before you, that He may keep and defend you. Seek Him for your security, who, living in the midst of the temptations of this city, will, but for His sustaining presence, fall as others have sadly fallen. Seek Him you who, in an age of controversy and keen intellectual rivalries, would know "the truth as it is in Jesus," that you may be more and more established in the faith once delivered to the saints. Seek Him yet again, you from whom He has departed. Pray Him to return—to come as once He came; to revive in you the better memories of the past—to enkindle within you once again the flame of that celestial fire. Cherish Him, if God grant your prayer, cherish Him as the Vestal virgins of old kept the sacred flame, ever bright and burning. Seek Him for your help, who know the secret happiness He always brings, that He may strengthen you for a still more active life in the service of your Master, that that great change of conversion may be more thorough and complete, that you may be renewed in the Spirit of your mind, that you may be so united by Him with Christ, that not death itself can separate you from Him.

Seek the Spirit of God reverently on your knees. Pray for His presence as you receive the Holy Communion. Praying thus He will surely be

E

vouchsafed to you. When others are weak, you will be strong. When others are downcast and desponding, you will be full of hope and joy. When the hands of others are idle, you will be full of good works, the fruit of the Spirit.

May that Spirit, poured forth as on this day, be shed abroad abundantly in your hearts! May your prayers be so answered, and your glad experience of His saving power be so great, that this shall be henceforth your one repeated, hearty desire:

"This God shall be our God for ever and ever. He shall be our guide unto death."

SERMON III.

THE STILLING OF THE TEMPEST.

St. Matthew viii. 26.

" And He saith unto them, Why are ye fearful,
O ye of little faith[1] ?"

THREE of the Evangelists record this miracle
of the stilling of the tempest, and with that
variety of detail which makes their threefold
and independent testimony the more valuable,
inasmuch as we infer from it the absence of any
collusion. Of the three versions, that of St.
Mark is the most minute and particular. It is
generally agreed that St. Mark's Gospel was
written at the dictation of St. Peter, who, being
one of the three chosen disciples of our Lord,
was always about His Person. St. Peter's testimony, therefore, is the testimony of an *eye-*
witness—of one who actually saw with his own

---

[1] Gospel. Fourth Sunday after the Epiphany.

E 2

eyes the facts which St. Mark narrates. Many
passages in St. Mark's Gospel, when compared
with the parallel accounts of the other Evangelists, confirm this opinion. It is not necessary to look further than St. Mark's account
of the stilling of the tempest, both to explain
my meaning and to illustrate the view generally entertained respecting his Gospel. Observe not only the minuteness of his description,
but how much that description betrays and
evidences the eye-witness. St. Matthew writes
thus: "there arose a great tempest in the sea,
insomuch that the ship was covered with the
waves." St. Mark writes: " there arose a
great storm of wind, and *the waves beat into the
ship, so that it was now full*" (ch. iv. 37).
St. Matthew simply says, "He was asleep."
St. Mark, "He was in the hinderpart of the
ship, *asleep on a pillow*." These are only two
of many similar instances of this evidence of
the *eye-witness* which abound in St. Mark's
Gospel [2].

Now it is important to notice this peculiar
feature in the Gospel of St. Mark, and to give

[2] Compare also St. Mark vi. 39, with St. Matt. xv. 35 ; xi. 4
with St. Matt. xxi. 2. St. Mark x. 46 is another instance of
the same.—*Townson on the Gospels*.

it its due weight. For it is of the nature of *internal evidence* for the authenticity of the Gospels. And by internal evidence is meant evidence apart and distinct from the history of the Gospel itself—evidence which the Gospels bear within themselves of their authenticity— evidence afforded by peculiarity of style, by undesigned coincidences, by consistency in me- thod of expression, by minute yet significant and unmistakeable features, which serve to identify one Gospel from another as readily as we recognize any modern author by the pecu- liarities of his style. From such minute and detailed description we may fairly argue that the Gospels of the New Testament are not for- geries. It is very improbable that it would occur to the mind of any one, purposing to write a false and mythical account, to enter into such minuteness of detail. On the other hand, this very minuteness indicates that the historian had been a spectator, on whose mind was imprinted the action which he had himself witnessed.

I have dwelt at some length on this point, because it is a branch of evidence not to be underrated or overlooked. The majority of trea- tises devoted to the consideration of the authen- ticity of the Gospels are occupied with the

external, direct historical evidence for the truth
of the Scriptures. Sufficient stress is scarcely
laid on those marks of truth, on that air and
language of reality which is no mean criterion
of authenticity, and which it is difficult, if not
impossible, to feign.

The situation, moreover, of this the most
sacred sheet of waters in the world, explains the
suddenness of the tempest, during which the
ship which bore the Saviour of mankind seemed
for a while in imminent peril.

The full significance of the words employed
by the Evangelists in the original text is to
some extent lost in the English translation.
St. Matthew employs a word expressive of this
suddenness, which strictly means *violent agitation*, as if by an earthquake (σεισμὸς being
the Greek for an earthquake). The word used
by St. Mark and St. Luke is another, viz.
λαίλαψ, i. e. *a violent squall, a sudden impetuous
whirlwind*, both however conveying the idea of
a *sudden* and unexpected storm.

Modern travellers who have visited the Holy
Land, agree in their description of the Lake of
Gennesareth, its scenery and physical features.
It is described as thirteen miles long, and in its
broadest part six miles wide, so that the form

which it generally presents is that of an oval. "That which makes it unlike any of our English lakes is the deep depression which gives it something of the strange unnatural character that belongs in a still greater degree to the Dead Sea, and in some degree to all lakes of volcanic origin[3]." The rocky walls of mountains and the sloping hills almost completely encircle it. This geographical feature is strictly in keeping with the Evangelists' description of the suddenness of the tempest, to which the Lake of Gennesareth, like every mountain lake, is more or less liable. The wind rushing through the mountain gorge and cleft ravine agitates the waters with a sudden gust, and with dangerous impetuosity.

It has been asked whether the sudden calm which ensued cannot be explained without resorting to any miraculous and supernatural intervention. Can it not be accounted for by the subjective apprehension of the disciples? "When Jesus awoke, and spoke calmly to them, His composure quieted their perturbed minds. A calm in the elements ensued, and they transferred the impression made upon their

---

[3] Stanley's "Sinai and Palestine," pp. 369, 370.

minds to nature." But consistently with the Scripture narrative such a theory cannot be admitted. It is propounded by the rationalistic school of interpretation, which would reduce all Scripture miracles to natural phenomena, and is therefore open to suspicion. As Neander truly remarks, "Christ must have known that the observers looked upon His words as *the cause* of the calm that ensued, and (bearing in mind His character) would not have employed a *deceit* to confirm their faith in His sovereignty, which, resting upon the foundations of truth, needed no such props as this [*]." Such a view would be utterly inconsistent and at variance with our idea of Him as the Verax— the very soul and fount of Truth. And when we read the detailed narratives of the Evangelists who record the miracle, and bear in mind the impression of reality which was evidently conveyed to their minds—when we mark the effect which it produced on those who witnessed it, who one and all unhesitatingly attributed the sudden calm to the Saviour's voice and the power exercised by Him as the Son of God, we can enter in some degree into the feelings of the

---

[*] " Life of Christ," p. 205.

traveller as he draws near and gazes for the
first time on a sheet of water associated with
the hallowing presence of our Lord, and the
scene of the exercise of His sovereign power
over wild and discordant Nature. "Cold must
be the heart," is the language of one writer,
"that throbs not with unwonted emotion [5]."
As the western hills stretch their lengthening
shadows over the lake, and the eye dwells upon it
in the calm and meditative hour of the still evening, we can well understand that sacred, solemn
awe which steals over the mind, as in imagination it endeavours to retrace His footsteps on
the shell-strewn beach, or to conjure up His form
amidst the calm still waters.

> " *There is nothing bright above, below,*
> *From flowers that bloom to stars that glow,*
> *But in its light my Soul can see*
> *Some feature of Thy Deity.*"

In our matter-of-fact age, my brethren, when
miracles such as these recorded in Scripture
have, as far as we know, ceased to be exercised,
—when we require that every thing shall be subjected to the severe and criticizing test of reason
and sense before we accept it,—when we regard

---

[5] Thomson, "The Land and the Book," p. 351.

with suspicion any alleged violation of or
departure from the ordinary operation of the laws
of Nature, and bring all phenomena under the
searching scrutiny of scientific investigation, it
is, perhaps, difficult to realize the fact that at the
simple command, " *Peace be still,*" the agitated
waters, threatening to sink the tempest-tossed
vessel, should have instantly subsided and settled
down into a dead, unruffled calm.   Such remarkable facts as these in the natural world do not
come within our own experience now, and
therefore there lurks in many minds, especially
with the more intellectual, a secret unbelief as to
their reality or possibility.   It may be that some
amongst us, as we have stood on the deck of a
vessel, trembling from stem to stern with the shock
of waves, which rising mountains high threaten
every moment to engulf her, have endeavoured,
looking out upon the wide expanse of the raging
sea, to picture to ourselves all that heaving ocean
hushed down into an instantaneous stillness by a
few spoken words.   May not the marvellous proofs
which we finite creatures witness of the triumphs
of Mind over Matter serve in some faint degree
to make this miracle more intelligible?   Do not the
more remarkable discoveries in every department
of Science, and the various uses which they are

made to subserve in this present age, attest and
illustrate the reality of this power amongst us?
What would our forefathers say were they to rise
from their graves, and be given to see how Time
and Space are almost annihilated, and how the
human mind exercised, brought to bear upon,
and, if I may so say, influencing dead, inert
matter, converts it into an obedient, willing
slave? Would not much, with the use and laws
of which we are conversant, seem to their duller
apprehension and less advanced knowledge, little
short of miraculous? And seeing this, shall we
deem it impossible that a Being of *infinite* power,
Who created all things, from Whose hand all
Nature sprang, could not perform on a grander
and more extended scale, what even we poor finite
creatures do on a smaller and more limited?
What are the laws of Nature and all the phenomena of Nature, but only another name for the
Will of God? If we believe in our hearts that
Christ is the Son of God, shall we say that any
thing is *impossible* with Him, because we do not
actually see with our own eyes the wondrous
incidents which studded His earthly life? If it
was necessary that, in the revelation of the Godhead, He should powerfully impress a belief in His
absolute sovereignty upon the minds of men by

certain visible exhibitions of it, does it not seem most fitting that He should do this in a manner most calculated to secure that end by an appeal to their senses ?   What more striking and convincing than that He should bid Nature in her wildest moods obey His Will, and confess to His power, whether over the disharmonies of our moral nature, as when He brought the demoniac to His feet in his right mind and restored reason, or when, in the calm majesty and dignity of His conscious Divinity, He woke out of that gentle and untroubled sleep, and, looking out on the angry tempest, bade it be still ?   Surely, surely, when we reflect on what the power of God is, how Omnipotent His sway, we ought not to limit it within the bounds of our finite capacity, nor narrow it by the experience of our own contracted sphere of being.

When we read of these miracles and meditate in this nineteenth century upon facts so extraordinary as these, we must bear in mind that they were not only necessary proofs of Christ's Divinity, as establishing His power to subjugate Nature, but that there is also a moral purpose intended by these manifestations.   The miracles of our Lord have always an ethical import in view. They are designed to teach us some particular lesson. It is this which we must chiefly consider—for it is this which more nearly concerns us. As there was an economy of miracles, no one of them unnecessarily or superfluously exercised, so we never find two miracles in the New Testament in all respects alike. Each and every one has its own lesson, serves a distinct purpose in that marvellous system of spiritual instruction contained in God's Word. It is this ethical purpose which serves to distinguish the miracles of Gospel history from the fables and legends of subsequent times. This one salient feature affords a criterion and test by which we are enabled to draw a sharp line of distinction between the miracles of Christ and such as were attributed to Him in spurious Gospels, or are palmed off in our own day upon a credulous crowd in the form of a winking Virgin, or a bleeding statue. In this miracle of stilling the tempest, Christ would lead His disciples into higher thoughts of Himself. He would teach them by this exercise of His power that in nearness to Him was safety and deliverance from danger. The stilling of the tempest is an image of the higher spiritual truth which Christ works in all ages, even that of speaking peace to every

believing soul amidst the storms and tempests of
our earthly life.

And more than this. We learn from it
that the danger which *exercises* faith should
strengthen faith. Our Lord does not rebuke
His disciples for being *without faith*. His
words are, " *O ye of little faith.*" They believed to a certain extent, but it was a weak
and imperfect faith. It failed them when they
most needed it. It was not strong enough to
repress the fears of the moment. It was not
equal to the trying occasion. Too easily was
their trust in God shaken. So long as the sky
over their heads was bright and sunny, and
scarce a breath of wind ruffled the untroubled
surface of the calm lake, and all peril was forgotten in conscious safety, their faith in Christ
was subjected to no rude, severe test. They
scarcely thought how weak it really was. But
when the heavens were darkened, and the howling
wind lashed the sea into fury, and wave after
wave beat into the ship, then the weakness of an
untried faith was shown in the alarm and terror
which possessed them, as they awoke Him out of
sleep with the cry, " Lord, save us : we perish."

This incident of Christ and His disciples in
the ship has ever been regarded as a symbol of

the Church of Christ.   It finds its counterpart in Old Testament history, in the Ark which bore Noah and his family safe midst the waters of the Deluge.   The image of the world as a great ship, of which God was at once the Maker and the pilot, was familiar to the Indians.   The same symbolic meaning lay in the procession of Egyptian priests bearing the sacred ship full of the images of the gods.   In early Christian art the Church is continually set forth as a ship against which the personified winds are fighting. The same idea has been engraved on an old seal ring, which was at one time one of the means employed by art to illustrate Scripture truths. Under all these images one and the same truth is symbolized, even this, the Church of Christ on earth exposed to dangers from without and to fears from within for its safety, yet preserved safe and unharmed because Christ is in it, —because that promise which He gave as He ascended into glory has been, and is still being fulfilled, *" Lo, I am with you alway, even unto the end of the world."*

Has it not ever been so in the past history of the Church?   Have there not been many and many critical periods, seasons of anxiety and trial, when the Church of Christ has been threat-

ened by a wide-spread spirit of infidelity from
without, or by error and heresy from within, and
has it not survived all these dangers, passed
safe through all these trials? Has it not
been miraculously preserved amidst the conflict
of adverse and hostile opinion? Has not the
season of lurid cloud and violent tempest been
always succeeded by one of stillness and rest and
calm?

Is not there a lesson in all this, brethren,
suited to the times in which we are living?
May we not learn something from the past which
ought to influence us, and weigh with us, and
quiet our minds, as we contemplate the aspect of
the religious world in our own day? We must
all feel that the Church of Christ is passing
through another of these critical periods in her
history. No one of any observation or education
can fail to notice this. The last few years have
been characterized, and will ever be, by an unusual spirit of theological controversy. Science
has made great strides. Modern research and
travel have opened up many questions bearing
upon Scripture which have to be reconciled with
God's Word as it is generally received. Geology,
Ethnology, Archæology, the study of Languages,
recent discoveries of supposed pre-Adamite races,

the questions these departments of knowledge and
research excite, threaten to create a revolution in
old and long-established belief. Works have been
written by professed Christian teachers which
strike at the very root of all our cherished opinions, and that by men whose position in the
Church naturally commands attention. A bold
and uncompromising criticism has been brought
to bear on the Old Testament, which indirectly
affects the New Testament also. Questions the
most important in connexion with religious
belief are freely and commonly discussed. Considerable agitation of a political character,
having reference to the connexion between
Church and State, the final Court of Appeal, and
kindred constitutional questions is going on
around us. This agitation from without, these
newly-broached opinions and hostile criticism
from within, justify us in saying that the
Church of Christ is passing through a season of
trial, through another great and momentous
crisis in her earthly history. Once again the
tempest is excited. We may hear the howling
of the wind. We may see the waves beating
into the ship. And once more a wide-spread
panic exists. It is a time confessedly of great
and prevailing religious disquietude. The

F

Christian world fears lest the ship should founder in the gale. We hear on all sides the echo of the disciples' terror-stricken cry, " Lord, save us : we perish."

But is there not also with us, as with the disciples, much unreasoning fear ? Is not our attitude and our frame of mind like theirs whom Christ reproved ? Does not this disquietude, this ill-disguised fear, this alarm, this anxiety for the safety of the Church betray our little faith in the overruling Providence of God, in the sure unfailing promise of Christ ? Do not we deserve the rebuke, " Why are ye fearful, O ye of little faith ?" True, the tempest rages round the ship, but is not Christ in it as of old? Is it so that any real danger exists? Is it not rather, that notwithstanding the religious activity of the day, *faith, real faith* is languishing amongst us ? May not this very activity, this multiplication of societies and associations be pushing faith out of place? and in our zeal for the extension of the Church of Christ by an increase in all external machinery and accessories, may we not be trusting too much to these, too little to that less showy, but more simple power which can remove mountains, and make all things possible to him that believeth ? Our

Lord, in founding His Church on earth, must have clearly foreseen all the influences, all the circumstances, all the means which in the course of ages would surround, attend, and be associated with its growth and development. With increasing knowledge, and with the appliances of modern times unknown to the Apostles, with the art of printing in such perfection, with our facilitated means of communication and locomotion, with all the apparatus of our highly civilized life, we enjoy superior advantages for circulating the Word of God, disseminating truth, and promulging Christianity, so far as this may be done by purely outward agency and means. All this may blind us, may deceive us into the idea that therefore, because so much religious zeal and activity exists, the Church of Christ must be taking deeper and deeper root in the world, and bringing forth more fruit. It may be no more than an unsuspected substitution of outward instrumentality for inward principle, a gradual supplanting of faith by the multiplication of more tangible means, and thus throwing much light and meaning on that far-seeing question which Christ asked, " When the Son of Man cometh, shall He find Faith on the earth?" Can we, nay rather *ought* we to doubt that as in times past God has safely brought His Church through seasons of peril, so now He will overrule this present crisis for good, and make the prevailing disquietude subserve His greater glory? Doubtless as He in His unerring wisdom permits a season of anxiety such as the present, so He would have it exercise and strengthen the faith which it tries. The exciting controversies of the day, the dangers of a too great latitudinarianism which threaten to remove the old landmarks of the Christian faith, should tend to strengthen rather than weaken it. These dangers challenge us to contend only the more earnestly for the faith once delivered to the saints. These passing fears excited by outward conflicting elements should make us more diligent students of the Holy Scriptures, should lead us to re-examine the grounds on which our belief *individually* rests, whether that belief be merely secondhand, the result of our religious instruction only, or grounded on personal conviction, on personal experience. Seasons such as these should bring us only the more often to our knees, in earnest and fervent supplication at the throne of grace for an increase of faith and for the high and blessed gift of the Holy Spirit

to illumine our understanding, to throw its own
instructive light on the sacred page, and to lead
us into all truth. Our faith, brethren, is of very
little practical worth if it gives way in the hour
when we most need it. It cannot be the result
of our own deep-rooted convictions. It wants the
very soul and life of true faith if we are easily
shaken by every wind of doctrine. It is not
worth much if a few blasts of error are strong
enough to uproot all the teaching of centuries'
growth; if some few objections, and these of
little or no practical importance, even if tenable,
suffice to excite a distrust in our minds of the
trustworthiness of that one Volume which is
"able to make us wise unto salvation through
faith which is in Christ Jesus."

Rather, therefore, than be unreasonably alarmed
and panic-stricken, lest that on which we are
each staking our soul's eternal interests should
be proved false or fallible, the fears excited by
the religious agitation are not to be regretted, if
they lead to the practical result of more frequent
study on our part, more believing prayer, more
humble faith in Christ. We shall have gained
something to the cause of truth, if when the
storm is past, and the waters have subsided once
more into a calm, and the sun breaks out again

in the heavens dark with the hanging clouds, we have learnt the weakness of our faith; if the danger which threatened our common belief has united us only the more closely to Christ, and established us the more firmly in the inspiring consciousness of His unseen yet real presence.

Such is the teaching of this miracle in its more general interpretation. It is applicable also to individual men in a more special sense. Poets frequently employ this image of a ship tempest-tossed, exposed to adverse storms and conflicting winds, as descriptive of human life and its troublous circumstances. We all recognize the force and truth of the image. The voyage of life towards Eternity, onward towards the wished-for haven of everlasting stillness and rest, is not, nor is intended to be, one of unbroken calm, of unruffled seas. Storms and tempests arise: how often without much or any previous warning! They come upon us, they overtake us when · least looked for or expected, like the sudden fitful gust of wind which, rushing through the mountain gorge, swept over the lake of Galilee. Who of us here has not known these, has not had some experience of them? Outward calamities, trials such as losses of friends or fortune, heartrending bereavements, bitter disappointments, oppressive anxieties, fretting, gnawing cares—these are storms from without. Have we not also known tempests from within, such as the suddenly excited power and strength of an unruly, unholy, turbulent, headstrong passion? Has not some temptation from without plied some sinful propensity within, and brought us to the very verge of wilful transgression? How often has our soul's eternal safety been imperilled through our almost yielding to the momentarily revived sinful habit, and in that mysterious striving of the Spirit with the fleshly lust, the lust has all but overcome the Spirit.

Have we not also been cast down by our spiritual fears—depressed, tortured, harassed by distressing doubts, by new forms of unbelief, by the remembrance of broken vows? Who of us, I repeat, has lived thus long and not known these buffetings from without, not felt the cruel power and tyranny of inward passion and sinful desires? Many amongst you, I doubt not, now advanced in years, can recall in your past life a season of trial and temptation. It may be that some here this morning are passing through such now. And you know how our hearts fail us in the day of earthly sorrow, anguish, and trial. You will not disguise from yourself the weakness of your faith amidst these trying circumstances. We do not endure " as seeing Him Who is invisible." We have too often and too quickly cried, "Lord, save us: we perish." Our fears, our despair, our restlessness, our impatience, our yielding to temptation have proved only too clearly our " *little faith*." Our belief in Christ has been no more, no deeper than the mere intellectual assent of the mind which is unequal to grapple with these mysteries of His spiritual kingdom. It is not the faith of those who cling closely to Him, driven to Him for shelter in the storm, consoled, and quieted, and strengthened by His sustaining, assuring presence. We have given way to undue fear, to excessive grief, to distressing doubt, or have fallen into sin, because our hearts are not habitually stayed upon Him, because we do not constantly live near to Him, because we have never yet really, heartily, without wavering, believed in Him. We have not taken in our hands and covered ourselves with that shield of faith which shall make us more than conquerors.

It is easy to believe in God in the day of prosperity, when all goes well with us, when

not a cloud overcasts the bright blue summer sky
of worldly happiness; but that is a stronger, more
enduring, more assuring, more reliable faith,
which can and does implicitly trust God in
adversity; that realizes His voice, His form, His
presence when the pelting rain and howling
wind and surging sea darken the heaven of our
souls. And is it not because they are lacking in
this lively and true faith, that we see men, otherwise courageous and strong, so easily cast down,
falling so readily into sin, unable to rise up
under the crushing sorrow, full of care and
anxiety, disturbed and without comfort in those
last moments of our mortal life, when in view of
the solemn change which awaits us, we ought to
have joy and peace in believing? Our blessed
Lord and Master would have men read in this
miracle that lesson of life that He is the speaker
of Peace to the troubled, storm-stirred spirit of
man, as well as to the tempests in the world of
nature. " The wicked are like the troubled sea
when it cannot rest, whose waters cast up mire
and dirt. There is no peace, saith my God, to
the wicked[6]." So we have read this morning.
For sinful and faithless souls there is no rest in

[6] Isa. lvii. 20, 21 (First Lesson).

life. Theirs is a troubled, chafing, reproaching conscience. They live in constant doubt and uncertainty, and disquieting fears. But they who live near Christ, and stay their minds on Him, and whose daily life corresponds with their belief, to such as these He is strength and safety.

Trials and temptations we are to expect, even though they come on us of a sudden and unawares. What we should seek and aim after is that habit of mind, that stablishing of our hearts, that habitual confidence and trust which shall find us spiritually pre-armed and prepared, that these trials when they come may strengthen our faith in exercising it, may not unduly cast us down. They should send us to our knees, not keep us from prayer. They should drive us into His presence, and to His throne of grace, supplicating for inward strength, relying on His gracious promise, which never fails, " As thy day, so shall thy strength be."

Nor ought we to give way, brethren, to the passions of our fallen nature, pleading the infirmity of our human nature as an excuse for sin, as if our passions cannot be controlled, as if we cannot bridle our lusts. We must not even plead our time of life or outward circumstances, as an apology for the vices of youth or manhood,

until we have tried and exhausted all those
sources of supernatural grace and strength which
are opened to earnest prayer, and which have their
fount and origin in Him Who hears and answers
earnest prayer. Christ's strength, remember, is,
made perfect in our weakness. When temptation
meets you, and Satan would, at any time, lead
you to do that which in your heart you know to
be displeasing in the sight of God, we should
utter some short ejaculatory petition as the
occasion suggests, that He " Who knows us to be
set in the midst of so many and great dangers,
that by reason of the frailty of our nature we
cannot always stand upright, would grant us
such strength and protection, as may support us
in all dangers, and carry us through all temptations [1]." Thus our faith would be strengthened
by its frequent exercise, and increased by trying
circumstances. For is it not so that his arm is
the most sinewy, the most strong and muscular,
which is constantly exercised ? Have not those
pine-trees taken the deepest root, where high up
on mountain top the storms rage in their wildest
fury ?

Rest we not satisfied, brethren, with that cold,

---

[1] Collect for the day.

dry, almost worthless degree of faith which consists in little more than the passive assent of the
mind to the fundamental truths of Christianity.
Remember rather to ask in your daily prayers
for an increase of active faith which shall give
life and reality and value to the truths in which
you believe; that faith by the power of which
our union with Christ is made more real and
more close. The one will only and surely fail
you in the hour of trial, the other will be the
sheet anchor of the soul, holding it fast and firm
when the storms arise.

Deep below the surface of the ocean there
flows a current calm and still. It is never
agitated by storm and tempest. The wind
ruffles not the even flow of that wave-
buried stream. So these our outward trials or
temptations will be but surface agitation, never
reaching the deeps of our being, if there be within
us the under-current of strong, settled, established
faith in Christ. In the Holy Communion, prepared for you this morning, you see a means of
thus drawing near to Christ. In that holy
ordinance He draws nigh to believing hearts.
So He has promised. So we believe. Are there
not some here who are in anxiety or sorrow,
weighed down with some earthly care, needing

His comfort and sustaining grace to stay their fainting spirit? Are there not some weak in themselves, of good resolutions, but of little power to keep them, contrite, yet fearing lest they should again fall into sin? As you draw near it, seeking strength and inward peace, surely we may believe that as of old He rose and bid the storm to cease on the sea of Galilee, so now He will, by the voice of His Spirit, speak to such amongst you the same words of quieting, assuring, consoling power,—" Peace, Peace, be still."

> " *Take courage, then, my soul, nor steep*
> *Thy days and nights in tears ;*
> *Thou soon shalt cease to mourn and weep,*
> *Though dark are now thy fears.*
> *He comes, He comes, the strong to save ;*
> *He comes, nor tarries more ;*
> *His light is breaking o'er the wave ;*
> *The clouds and storms are o'er* [3]*."*

[3] " Lyra Germanica."

SERMON IV.

PRACTICAL RELIGION.

1 Peter iii. 15.

" Sanctify the Lord God in your hearts¹."

There exists an unreasonable prejudice with
many against that class of discourse which is
occupied with the cultivation and improvement
of character as its theme, or with the enforce-
ment of the practice of those virtues which have
for their befitting and especial sphere of exercise,
the more extended of our general intercourse
with mankind, or the more limited of domestic
life. Sermons of this nature are for the most
part invidiously designated " moral essays," more
suitable to the dispensation of a past Theism,
and as belonging to Natural Theology, than in
keeping with the essential characteristics of the

¹ Epistle, Fifth Sunday after Trinity.

Christian revelation, or as forming an element of a more enlightened creed.

There are not a few pious persons who express themselves dissatisfied with that exposition of Scripture, or of any particular text, which does not either embrace the whole circle of Christian truth, or at the least enlarge upon certain distinctive doctrines connected with it. With such, Articles of faith, orthodoxy of belief, correct views, sound teaching, are regarded of such prime importance and all-absorbing interest, that the attention is but seldom directed to that, which must be the best and only criterion of our faith, viz. the real influence which religion possesses with the man himself, and the controlling power it is permitted to exercise over the conduct and demeanour in all the varied circumstances of his public or private life.

Nor is that expositor tolerated, or his teaching considered true to the genius of the Gospel, who, from time to time as opportunity may present itself, or circumstances require, takes for his subject of pulpit treatment the various developments and phases of character with which we are being continually brought into contact, more especially such as have necessarily a direct and intimate bearing upon society at large. To all practical purposes these which more than aught else—more than formally-repeated Litanies, or ostentatious almsgiving, or frequent attendance at the house of God, give significant evidence of the presence or absence of religious principle, are kept in the background, or considered as of very secondary moment.   Religion is thus made to consist more in orthodoxy than in practice; more in clear and settled views on abstruse questions than in the every-day demeanour; more in an implicit faith in all the dogmas of revelation, than in the spirit, and tone of mind, and general bearing in which we associate with and act one towards another in the daily life.   Men are not unfrequently more anxious to be sound theologians than consistent Christians; to be well versed in the arguments of conflicting schools of opinion and the subtleties of controversy, than to have their walk on earth with God; and in their laudable desire that the name of Christ should be exalted above every name, and the blessings of redemption proclaimed, and the all-sufficiency of His atonement preached in every sermon, in opposition to any idea of human merit, they are in danger of losing sight of the bright example He ever sets before us of an holy life, and how noble an illustration He was in

His own person of all those virtues which most adorn and dignify character.

Doubtless a religion of doctrines is far less requiring than one which insists on the cultivation of character. Where persons are not in the habit of exercising the intellect, or given to much deep thought, or averse to too minute an inquiry into the nature and objects of faith, because of the inscrutable mystery which overhangs and envelopes the truths of revelation, a ready acquiescence in the creed into which they have been baptized, and an assent to its several articles is both natural and unrequiring. A vast proportion of the adherents to any branch of the Christian Church, or of any particular sect, owe their adhesion more to the force of the associations in which they have been nurtured, to the early education they have received, with all the deep-rooted prejudices which are originated and fostered in childhood, and, above all, to the fact that their own is the persuasion which they have inherited from ancestors, than from any deep-settled, intelligent conviction of its truth or Scripture warrant. The mere fact, therefore, of our belonging to this or that denomination must be always an uncertain and unsatisfactory crite-

rion.   Indeed it is no criterion whatever.   It
must be obvious that religion, as well as philosophy, admits of theory.   Theory may exist apart
from practice.   *Christian* does not necessarily
imply a true disciple of Christ Jesus.   It may
be no more than the nomenclature or badge
by which we are distinguished from a Maho-
medan, Hindoo, or Socinian.   The outward profession or adherence may be quite distinct from
any studied regard for the obligations of such
profession.   Texts of Scripture may be readily
learned by rote, and be aptly quoted; the few,
precious, saving truths may be embraced; there
may be a pious horror of Romanism, and a praiseworthy zeal for Protestant truth; yet, co-existing
with all this, there may be blemishes of character
to a degree lamentable; sins indulged in, which
belie all profession; infirmities of temper, telling
of a want of self-discipline; habits of indolence
or intemperance, which have a directly pernicious
tendency, and a disposition exhibited in the
transactions of business, in our social intercourse, in the expression of opinion, and in the
tone of our conversation when particular restraints are withdrawn, which clearly show that
whatever we may *believe,* our belief does not

produce as its direct result that which is implied in the text, " Sanctify the Lord God in your hearts."

Yet surely Christianity, and the scheme comprehended by it, was never designed to supersede the necessity of all which, before its introduction into the world, was revealed and regarded as necessary on the part of moral beings, with a view to their obtaining the favour of the Most High. It cannot have relaxed the stringency of the moral law, wherever that law was concerned with great fundamental principles of conduct, nor have rendered certain affections and states of the heart less imperative than before. Neither was it ever contemplated that henceforth religion should be a matter of faith only, and not one which should be concerned with the whole, diversified, and extensive domain of man's moral and spiritual being. " Christianity," as Bishop Butler writes, " is a republication and external institution of natural or essential religion, adapted to the present circumstances of mankind, and intended to promote natural piety and virtue." It has, as the same writer goes on to show, a still further purpose, as containing a " revelation of a particular dispensation of Providence, carrying on by His Son and Spirit, for the recovery and salvation of mankind, who are represented, in Scripture, to be in a state of ruin." This however, its distinctive object, does not require that we should ignore all former teaching, nor does it suppose that the cultivation of character in this our state of probation is of little or no moment. On the contrary, morality, and all which is generally understood by this term, has met with its highest expression in Him, Whom even men the most hostile to Christianity confessed as in all things irreproachable. Every virtue, every quality of mind, every trait of character which we instinctively appreciate and admire, was exhibited in the person of our Redeemer. And is it not so, that whenever you read the record of His most holy life, and call to mind the trying circumstances in which He was often situated,—the subtle nature of the temptations which were presented to Him,—the opportunities deliberately thrown in His way, in order that in an unguarded moment He might commit some indiscretion,—the many incidents which might naturally be expected to provoke Him to anger, or to betray into hastiness of resentment one less on his guard than He, on each and every occasion you find that He acted

in strict conformity and harmony with those
eternal principles, which form the foundation
and basis of character, and herein has set us an
example that we should follow His steps? Have
you not often observed how seldom our blessed
Lord enunciated new truths, or encouraged
speculative inquiry, or gave room, further than
was absolutely necessary, for discussion on
points of faith? Rather, was not His own life
on earth one consistent with the idea of Revelation,—one of daily, hourly instruction in that
which lies more immediately within the compass
of our finite understanding? Did He not teach
man by the force of His own illustrious example
the lessons of true religion? Did He not display, as imaged forth in Himself, the principles
on which we should act, proving that it is possible so to act ? Did He not show us of what
Humanity is capable; under and through what
assistance we may regain something of our pris-
tine integrity; how even on this earth, now
the theatre of Satan's permitted dominion,
and like some once fair garden upon which the
blight of sin has fallen, we may vindicate the
holiness of God ; how we may ourselves be witnesses to our more pure and celestial origin ; how
we may overcome the evil which surrounds us

by the superior influence of a saintly life, and make manifest to all around us the excellences of that inward disposition which arises from sanctifying the Lord God in our hearts?

I shall not be misunderstood in these remarks. A right faith is, beyond all controversy, of first and chiefest importance. As beings destined for an immortal existence, it must obviously be of the utmost consequence that we understand rightly the nature of the conditions which our Creator has indissolubly connected with future happiness, and on which alone we can reasonably expect to share in those privileges which are reserved for such as obey His commandments. It is of the last moment to each individual member of this congregation that he believes savingly in Jesus Christ as the propitiation for sin, as "made unto us wisdom, and righteousness, and sanctification, and redemption;" that he also recognizes the work of the Spirit, as the only sanctifying and regenerating influence, and the absolute necessity of having a changed heart. Our first care should ever be, that ours is a well-grounded hope for the future; that the creed to which we give our assent, and on which we stake our deepest interests, be consistent with reason and agreeable to Scripture; that

the Book by which we regulate our lives, and
which we adopt as our guide, be authenticated
by the most indisputable evidence as the inspired Word of God, and that we be always
ready to give an answer to every man that
asketh a reason of the hope that is in us. But
truths such as we believe in, holy and exalted
as they are, are not proposed to us merely
for our passive contemplation, or as exercises
for the intellect, or as facts in the world's moral
history. Meditation upon them ought to produce
in us various emotions, awaken impressions, and
suggest reflections, which shall cause us to
institute, almost involuntarily, comparisons between the absolute holiness of God and our oft-
experienced sinfulness; between His purity and
our impurity; between the perfect character of
Christ, as exhibited throughout His life on
earth, and our own many frailties, faults, and
infirmities; between the outgoings of a mind
possessed of the Holy Ghost and one yet
worldly, unspiritual, and dead to any vivid
perception of eternal truth. And these comparisons must produce yet further and more practical results. Example must suggest imitation.
A high standard should quicken us to earnest
endeavours to attain, as near as possible, to it :

so that conduct shall be the criterion of our faith. We must be "living epistles read of all men." Our light must so shine before men, that they may see our good works, and glorify our Father which is in Heaven. For what is it which so recommends Christianity? What is it that is in itself evidence of its Divine origin? Is it not the purity of its teaching—the seal which it sets to our purest instincts—the harmony which it establishes between the abstract idea of holiness, and those first principles of morality which all men allow, even where they do not themselves observe them? And by what do we judge of one another, and by what are we in turn judged? The crowd amongst whom we move is ignorant of the nature of our religious convictions. Men do not ask to what degree we believe or disbelieve. They do not question us, in our intercourse with them in the different relationships of life, as to what our opinion may be on this or that mooted subject, or on a particular article of faith, and then form their estimate of our character or moral worth from the opinion we express. They do not call and regard us as Christians, merely because we believe in a common Saviour, and have been baptized into the Church of Christ. No. The world, your friends and acquaintance, your children, your servants judge of the degree to which you are a religious man or woman, by that which they witness in your daily deportment. They judge of us by incidents, some so trifling, that they scarcely admit of being mentioned here, and yet singly or in the aggregate, deeply significant. There is an intuitive quickness to discriminate between hypocrisy and sincerity; between mere talk about religion, and real piety; between the mere outward show— "the leaves" of appearance—and true, deep-seated, religious principle. You can readily tell whether religion is assumed for a purpose, without any serious conviction of the obligations it imposes on such as profess it, or whether the man is seeking, to the best of his ability and under the assistance of the Holy Spirit, to sanctify the Lord God in his heart.

It is but very rarely, if indeed ever, that we are called upon to give such proofs of our sincerity and of the reality of our convictions, as shall be sufficient to establish at once, and by one courageous act, our undoubted honesty. Persecutions are unknown amongst us. The fires of a cruel bigotry are happily extinguished. We run no risk of martyrdom in the cause of

religion.   Yet there are other and not less
infallible means, by which the strength of our
religious principle is frequently tested—points
in which men are never hypocrites, because they
are not on their guard, and unlooked-for circumstances occur to develope the character.   These
reveal the secret disposition more faithfully often
than any more direct or searching test.

Scarcely a day passes in which we have not
opportunity for belying our profession or for
exhibiting the genius and spirit of Christianity.
Scarcely an hour is spent, in which the inveterate enemy of our souls does not tempt us into
an expression of opinion which, on maturer
reflection, we regret we should have uttered,
into hastiness of judgment or uncharitable remarks, which the more frequently they are made,
do violence to every better feeling and prove
our deficiency in vital Christianity.   Thus we
are always on our trial.   It is not as if we
could invariably and systematically disguise our
real sentiments and under all circumstances act
a part.   The prevailing, peculiar disposition or
propensity will be constantly excited, and if we
have not the power of self-control—if our words
and thoughts be not subjected to wholesome
discipline, we shall be betrayed, when we least

expect it, into inconsistencies and into conduct at variance with our profession. So that we have always to be on our guard. Men who are proof against the seductive enticements of grosser sins are often unequal to resist those more delicate which insinuate themselves into friendly conversation, and into the circles of our social life. Many who are scrupulous in all matters of external observance, and to all appearance ruled by a fear of God, were they to review the incidents of one week, to recall the scenes in which they moved, the conversations in which they bore a part, the opinions they expressed, would find that there was often a great want of charity, of brotherly love, of consideration for the failings or infirmities of others. They would have reason to censure themselves for their readiness to take offence; for the absence of proper self-restraint under provocation; for the unchecked impulses of resentment; for a harshness and unnecessary warmth of temper which was as fuel to the kindled fire of anger; nay more, they might often condemn themselves for a bearing and deportment towards one of inferior position, unbecoming to a Christian man and arguing the presence of a pride hateful in the sight of God.

Are these points, think you, of little moment? Are they such as have no place in Christianity? Is no provision made in the Gospel for a due control over self? Are there no higher laws or more sacred precepts to be discovered in the New Testament, which may be brought to bear upon these, the details indeed of life, but details, be it well remembered, which enter largely into the relationships of our social condition here? Reflect how much of the happiness or misery of life arises from attention to, or a disregard for the peculiarities of our fellow-creatures. There is often a reckless and wanton disparagement of that which has excited our envy; or an indisposition to put a favourable construction upon actions which others applaud; or to attribute genuine motives for a particular course of conduct. Often, amongst so-called Christians, words of guile are spoken on occasions when the scandal could not at once be met by an indignant denial, or inuendos are thrown out which invariably give rise to yet graver suspicions; false aspersions are cast in secret upon a fair reputation, which, like some of those deadly poisons for which no test or remedy is known, rankle in the heart, inflame the blood, and change the friend of years into the estranged and distant acquaintance—sometimes into the bitter foe.

How much of the disunion which unhappily exists in families, and of the positive animosity on the part of members of the same household toward one another, might be traced up to some such exciting and apparently trifling cause; to some calumny, or idle remark; some unguarded expression, or thoughtlessly-repeated opinion; some comment, exaggerated by repetition, until it became invested with a meaning which it was originally never intended to convey, and which now it is almost impossible to refute or forget. So close are the ties by which we are bound to each other; so complicated and delicate the threads of the great law of Sympathy; so much lies in our power, as individuals, for the promotion and maintenance of mutual happiness, that religion, to be of any real, practical value, must be of such a nature that it can be concerned with these, the minor details of conduct, and such as can be brought to bear upon the particulars of a man's thoughts, and words, and actions.

Have you not occasionally been brought yourself in contact with one whose unostentatious piety and consistency of conduct has exercised an irresistible influence upon the conversation and opinions of all who were present—one, who without display or obtrusiveness, exhibited all the characteristics of practical religion—whose presence operated as a charm, because you felt that you would meet with no sympathy or encouragement in any thing which was inconsistent with true religion? Have you not known one who was evidently possessed of the Spirit of God, breathed forth in kindness and brotherly charity,—in whose hands you knew that your honour and reputation were safe; who never spoke evil, but always sought for some palliative or excuse; who bore provocation without resentment, and injury without vindictiveness,—the foremost to soothe excited anger, and the first to counsel reconciliation; who rendered not evil for evil, or railing for railing, but overcame evil with good—one whose religion was not confined to outward observances, but who used these as means of sustaining the hidden life, and who humbly endeavoured to carry out into the sphere of active life, in business, in society, in all the refinements of mutual intercourse, the great principle expressed in the passage of Scripture, " Sanctify the Lord God in your hearts ? "

Is it not, moreover, a matter of your own

experience how much of the comfort of life depends on our own disposition, or on that of those with whom we live? How very slender a circumstance may embitter or gladden existence! In the most tender connexions it may require much of a gentle and yielding spirit to adapt ourselves to the peculiarities of another. Where this disposition exists, we shall soon learn to bear and forbear. We shall understand, and take pains how we may avoid the look, the gesture, the allusion, which would certainly excite or annoy. We must make the same allowance which we in turn expect from others, for those differences of taste, disposition, and habit, which are the result frequently of education, or of a particular calling, or of associations of early years, or of influences to which we have been subjected, and which have had a particular effect upon us. To make these allowances; to have this spirit diffused throughout our whole conduct; to be charitable, forbearing, forgiving, this is more requiring, and calls for more real thwarting of our own will, more habitual self-control, than formal prayers, and acts of routine devotion, and stated moments of seriousness. And more than the *comfort* of life depends upon the possession of this spirit. We are *more useful* in proportion as it is ours. It is not only in great and glorious deeds, which shall attract the admiration of the world and hand down our name to future generations, that we may be useful. The vast ocean excites our wonder, it bears upon its bosom the world's commerce, but we cannot spare the presence of one of the many fertilizing rivers and silent streams which flow on in their own gentle and quiet beauty. It is so with Life. There are great and honoured names which we reverence; representative men, who express all that is most noble and worthy of our esteem. But all have not the same opportunity. Some have a more extended, others a more limited sphere of usefulness. Some talents require a larger field for their proper development, some are only, but especially, suited to a less extensive area. Some men are gifted with a power of mind, or vigour of intellect, or other distinction, which shall benefit the whole human race; others, with these in a degree which must look for no greater influence than in their own home. It is so in the world of nature. There are mighty forces around us, on the constancy and regularity of whose operations the universe exists. There are also agencies of a less potent character, too minute for the unaided sight to discover, whose presence could not be spared in the economy of Creation. And if it be not given to us to have a position which commands, or talents which insure an almost universal influence, we can all of us cultivate at least the gentler charities. We may, and ought to endeavour, so far as in us lies, by a consistent walk to benefit, and be of some real good to those with whom we are connected by the ties of kindred, or other bonds of union. We are to preach Christianity and proclaim its excellence in our own homes. We should endeavour to show forth in our private home-life the evidence of a mind that is in all things influenced by the Spirit of God.

We must also bear in mind that it is only by this that men can form any opinion of the nature of religion. Few are theologians. Fewer still care for opinions which have no influence upon practice. It is not by great deeds under trying circumstances that men judge of the Gospel of Christ. It is comparatively rarely that we are placed in those circumstances. False religions can point to martyrs who have embraced death. It is rather when we are off our guard—when we least suspect the difference which at the moment a fear of God, or forgetfulness of Him, would cause in our conduct, it is when we are led on by conversation to speak of others, or are interested in some subject which is capable of being materially affected by the spirit in which we discuss it—these are opportunities continually recurring, in which the temptation lies to be inconsistent, and occasion is afforded for an exhibition of the genius of true piety. It is in the fulfilment of ordinary, familiar, commonplace duties that religion is susceptible of the brightest illustrations, or liable to be brought into contempt. The husband cannot be indifferent to the gentle spirit of his wife, nor the wife to the temper of her husband. The brother and sister living under the same roof, may make their home one of a happiness to which, in the after stormy scenes of life, memory shall revert with pleasure, or one of daily wrangling and unseemly discord. The child, ignorant altogether of disputed doctrines, and understanding nothing of the faith into which it has been baptized, receives insensibly its earliest impressions for good or for evil from the influences which surround it, and even in childhood forms no very erroneous estimate of the value of religion, by that which it sees in the conduct of its parents. And servants, who often, it is to be feared, in the world of fashion, enjoy few and rare opportunities for the cultivation of religion, and who are debarred from the use of many spiritual advantages by the inconsiderate demands made upon them by those whom they serve—these, as they wait upon us, are constant observers of our deportment. They have access to our privacy. We expect of them that they should conform to the rules and habits of the family. They overhear our conversation. They see us as we are when certain restraints are withdrawn, and when we forget to be artificial. Is it not, therefore, at once apparent how responsible we are for the example which we set them, and how very deeply that example may affect their future?

My brethren, the gist of the whole matter lies in this: " Sanctify the Lord God in your hearts." Carry about with you a constant recollection of His presence. Remember—remember—that His eye is ever resting upon you. Remember that Satan, that great, inveterate enemy of your soul, is never, never still—watching for every opportunity, ever giving occasion in which you may dishonour the religion you profess. Aim not so much to be remarkable in the world for virtues which may dazzle by their splendour; rather desire so to have in all things the mind of Christ, and so to move amongst

H 2

men, that you shall be known and respected as a consistent Christian. Morality, social virtue, call it by what name you please, has received its highest sanction in the character of our Redeemer. Step by step our characters are formed—by a slow and painstaking process, it is true—but the Christian character is that which will be selected hereafter. No care, therefore, to perfect it can ever be considered too great. Delay not the effort until it be too late. It carries with it its own reward, in the influence which it cannot fail, sooner or later, to exercise—in the reflex power it possesses to lend to life a secret charm and happy colouring. "The eyes of the Lord are over the righteous, and his ears are open unto their prayers." A sacred reverence for all things in which His name or honour is concerned; a jealous regard for those great, eternal principles—Truth, Justice, Love:—these recommend us in the sight of Heaven—these, through the merits and intercession of Christ, make our prayers acceptable and our praises grateful. Endeavour —strive to live as far as possible up to the spirit of the Epistle which has been read to you this morning. Take it, sentence by sentence, word by word, and compare your own daily life with the precepts it enjoins. Not now only, under

these circumstances of solemnity, but when the
service is ended, pray in your own room with
fervency of supplication for that gift from on
high, which can alone enable you so to walk
and to please God. Pray under a deep conviction of your own infirmities and many short-
comings. Pray with the earnestness of one
who, living though he be in the midst of a
sinful world, is above all things desirous to in-
herit the blessing of the righteous; and, through
the all-sufficient merits of our ascended Lord,
to be accepted hereafter as meet for the presence
of God, and of the spirits of just men made
perfect in glory.

" *If on our daily course, our mind*
Be set to hallow all we find,   .
New treasures still, of countless price,
God will provide for sacrifice.

" *The trivial round, the common task,*
Will furnish all we ought to ask,
Room to deny ourselves,—a road
To bring us daily nearer God.

" *Only, O Lord, in Thy dear love*
Fit us for perfect rest above;
And help us, this and every day,
To live more nearly as we pray."

SERMON V.

PROVERBS x. 7.

" The memory of the just is blessed."

OUR CHURCH, my brethren, commemorates at this season of the year the faithful who have departed this life.   In the Festival of All Saints, celebrated yesterday, we retain what we believe to be the teaching of Scripture respecting the dead, teaching free from superstition and agreeable to reason.   In observing this Festival we are committed to no opinion other than such as is founded on rational conviction and confirmed by Revelation.   Dogmatic teaching on a subject so obscure and mysterious as that of the state and condition of the departed is both unauthorized and presumptuous.   We have no positive information to justify dogmatism, and the hints which the Bible affords are of too general a character to allow of more than conjecture and surmise.

So long as we confine ourselves within the limits which reason and Revelation alike prescribe, the subject is one peculiarly interesting in itself, and calculated to encourage salutary and profitable reflections. So soon as we trespass beyond these limits, seek to be wise above that which is revealed, and indulge a prying curiosity, no limit can be placed to the fanciful and irrational theories which a highly wrought and imaginative mind, disregarding logic, common sense and Scripture, will form, and the foolish speculations in which it will riot and indulge.

This is one of those subjects which does not admit of much or wide difference of opinion. The data are but few by which we are enabled to arrive at any conclusion, and these data are common to us all. The facts, the additional facts we should require to justify us in dissenting from the general conviction, or in claiming superior knowledge, are such as we have no means of procuring. They are of a nature which renders it absolutely impossible that we should expect information, intentionally withheld from us in this our probationary state. In other departments of knowledge to which additions are being continually made, one man may surpass another by the discovery which he has brought to light in the laboratory, as the result of his studies and experiments. He may elicit new and fresh facts, and thus establish a claim to superior information. There is no such limit imposed in the acquisition of knowledge, regarded in a purely scientific point of view, as there is with reference to the condition of the departed. Here we meet with an insuperable barrier. A veil of mystery screens the living from the dead. A veil which no mortal hand can raise, no mortal eye can penetrate. Our faculties are unequal to the superhuman exercise of tracking the soul in its viewless flight when it quits the earthly tabernacle of the flesh. Our powers of vision fail us when we would see that world—if another world it really be—into which the spirit of man travels when he breathes his last, and the regions into which it passes hence for ever. Our sense of hearing is too faint and dull to detect a sound or voice in the stillness of the solemn midnight hour, or under circumstances of quiet and solitude when, if at any time, echoes from the

unseen world might break upon the ear. When
we commit a fellow-creature to the grave we
know that his body returns to its kindred dust.
The outward physical organism which consti-
tuted the tenement of the soul is resolved into
its original elements. For the present, at least,
it is divorced from the soul. It has no longer
any visible, material connection with it. It
undergoes such a change that in the course of
a few years scarcely a trace of it may be discovered. The place knoweth us no more.
Meanwhile where the soul is—whither it has
sped and gone—into what new scenes it has
passed—under what conditions it exists—in
what form and association, of this we are
almost entirely ignorant. Philosophy cannot
solve the enigma. Science cannot unravel the
mystery. We dare not trust our imagination.
The only idea we have of a spirit—that is
at all within our comprehension—is in its association with an outward, material organization,
through and by which it operates, and on which
it seems to be, to a great degree, dependent.
We are accustomed to think of a spirit as of
something which has a local presence and is in
intimate union with the physical nature of man.
Any other idea of it is beyond our conception,

or is at least too vague and abstract for the finite understanding. Death interrupts, dissolves this union. In a moment, in the twinkling of an eye, the silver cord of life is loosed. It is an instantaneous severance. There is nothing more so. And then what a change of condition soul and body severally undergo! The body, bereft of life, lies cold—inanimate—speechless. It is dead to all around it; dead to friendship, and unmoved by the tears of weeping friends; dead to joys and cares; dead to pain and pleasure; dead to the pursuits and interests of life; dead to the world which buries it quickly out of sight and mind. And the soul that gave it its life and animation and impulses has passed away—has passed away!

These are facts familiar to us all. They are painful and harassing to contemplate. Still, our information does not extend much beyond them. As regards actual locality, condition, and faculties, we know little positive or certain respecting the spirits of the dead. We know enough indeed for all practical purposes to console us under bereavement, and to quiet our minds in the prospect of dissolution. We know enough to make prayers to the dead unwarranted and superstitious. This also we know, that though removed from these terrestrial scenes in which they once took their part, removed beyond sight and hearing, that "they are blessed which die in the Lord from henceforth : yea, saith the Spirit, that they may rest from their labours²."

Here then, my brethren, is a limit clearly defined, which does not recognize, sanction, or even tacitly countenance so-called Spiritualism. To have any further information we must have new, well-authenticated facts, free from all doubt and suspicion, and such as shall be in harmony with reason and the general tenour of Scripture. They must moreover be of a nature clearly supernatural, not susceptible of any other interpretation, nor to be accounted for on any hypothesis which would explain the phenomena irrespective of any supernatural element. Whoever lays claim to additional knowledge concerning the spirit world, must first secure our assent by adducing proofs of his statements which shall do no violence to common sense, and shall be in accordance with established and recognized principles respecting the mutual dependence

² Rev. xiv. 13.

of soul and body, and of that connection essential, so far as we can see, to activity and locomotion. These are broad and general grounds on which to base our argument. They cannot well be objected to as unreasonable, too limited, or unfair.

The advocates of Spiritualism require of us that we should accept as facts, phenomena which do not comply with these conditions. The so-called " manifestations " are at variance with notions founded on common experience. They set at nought recognized principles, and necessitate a complete revolution of ideas with reference to the nature of spirit. It is no longer something immaterial in its essence, fine and subtle, ethereal, imperceptible to sight, impalpable to the organ of touch—it may be brought into immediate and conscious contact with our senses. It has not passed away from these lower terrestrial scenes—it only waits to be invoked to attest its nearness. It has not entered into a state of rest, removed from all that can harass or disturb it—it must be ready to obey the summons of the privileged " medium." It is not even at liberty to manifest itself at will, but is restrained by such conditions as the humour, temper, and inclination of

the "medium." It is not in the tranquil
possession of that freedom from every human
anxiety and every human care, which we are
elsewhere taught to believe the soul, when freed
from the burden of the flesh, enjoys—it is
continually vexed by the importunity and ques-
tionings of its living friends. It manifests its
presence by feats of physical strength, which in
its lifetime it would have hesitated so much as
to attempt. It indulges in freaks of a playful
and undignified nature. It performs marvels
which reduce the laws of gravitation to a positive absurdity. So far from moving in the
presence of God, and being safe in the keeping
of Jesus, awaiting the judgment day, and
associated, as we should imagine, with all that
is of most solemn circumstances and full of
awful interest, it may readily be evoked from
the regions of the departed to minister to the
recreation and amusement of an evening circle
—to be questioned on matters of the most
solemn or most trivial character, without sug-
gesting one feeling of awe, and not unfrequently exciting laughter. To all inquiries
concerning the future, the spirit replies with
a commendable caution, with an ambiguity
worthy of the Pythian priestess or the Sybil of

Cumæ, lest the prediction might haply prove untrue. The more astute repudiate the gift of prescience and the power of foretelling events. They can give no information concerning the past that may not be otherwise learned. As regards the present, their replies are enigmatical and obscure. In point of fact, they knew more when they were with us than they know now in that world "where we shall know even as we are known."

"*Cui bono?*" is the practical question which may fairly be applied to so-called Spiritualism. It is a subject of high pretensions; it challenges public attention. Some practical test must be applied to establish its reality or to expose its falsity. This test is at once fair and unexceptionable. The question at issue is not so much whether Spiritualism is of Satanic origin and agency. It is rather a question of fact. Is Spiritualism a reality, or is it not? May its phenomena be satisfactorily explained without having recourse to an interpretation which implies the supernatural? May they be no more than the figments of imagination or the clever tricks of a consummate conjuror? The question even as to whether it be right or wrong to take part in a "*séance*" cannot be answered until·

the more important point is settled. We may not even in every case be able to account for facts which our own eyes have witnessed, and which appear supernatural. We are not therefore necessarily committed to the belief that they are supernatural. We may not be able at once to detect the imposition and expose the deception. We are not therefore identified with all the anomalies and inconsistencies of the theory itself. It were most illogical and indeed unfair, to regard as a convert one who attends a *séance* from the reasonable desire to judge for himself, and to subject the phenomena to certain searching tests.

Applying to Spiritualism the " *cui bono* " test, we may assert, without fear of contradiction, that as yet it has added nothing to our knowledge. There is no subject on which it has thrown any new light. No department of science has been enriched by it. It has revealed no truth of an important and practical nature, bearing on the temporal or spiritual interests of man, with which we are not already conversant. Granted that it is a reality, what distinct purpose does Spiritualism propose to itself or serve? The ethical element is entirely wanting. The criteria by which we discriminate between a

true and a spurious miracle, between the miracles
of the canonical and those of apocryphal Gospels, may fairly be applied to this subject also.
As any high purpose and aim is clearly altogether absent from the latter, and serves as a
mark by which to distinguish them from those
which had always some prominent ethical significance, so it is with regard to the manifestations of Spiritualism. They are without a
moral. They have and aim at no such distinct
teaching as shall give them even the air of
truth and reality[s]. If the spirits of the departed are really permitted of God to hold such
intercourse with men on earth, as spiritualists
maintain that they do, then it is almost in-
credible that their information should be so
meagre and scanty. We are at a loss to account
for the fact that they should not also be permitted to satisfy our curiosity on many points
connected with the after state. If once the
natural hindrances could be removed, which
we are in the habit of supposing effectually
forbid the idea of any communication with
spirits, then the restraint and reserve, which
they notoriously maintain, is inconsistent in the

[s] Vide Trench on "The Miracles of the Apocryphal Gospels." "Notes on Miracles," p. 39, fourth edition.

extreme, seeing that the only possible reason
that we can conceive for such permission being
given, is not to gratify mere idle, prurient
curiosity, but, surely, for some higher and
better purpose. But as a matter of fact and
of common experience, no good has as yet been
attained through or by spiritual manifestations;
no such good as to make us desire to see Spiritualism encouraged; no such good as to outweigh the evils which may result from it, not
the least of which is that morbid, unhealthy
curiosity, which Scripture tacitly rebukes.

If, as its advocates confidently affirm, un-
believers have been led, through the influence
of Spiritualism, to believe in the immortality of
the soul, where before they doubted or denied it,
it does not argue much for the intelligence of
their converts if they cannot distinguish between immortality and immateriality, or understand that there is no necessary connexion
between these two ideas. The utmost that
these manifestations could prove, supposing
them actually to occur, would be the existence
of the soul in a separate state. But the fact of
the soul being immaterial, and of its separate
existence, does not necessarily prove it to be
immortal. This is too evident to require any

I

elaborate reasoning. So far from proving the Immortality of the soul, they would be arguing on weak and fallacious grounds. The Deity might at His will annihilate mind and reduce the whole universe to nothing, and though He has nowhere given any intimation, tacit or expressed, that may lead us to believe His intention of destroying the spirit, yet we could not urge the immateriality of the soul as an irrefragable argument for its immortality, so long as the power of the Deity is admitted as absolute [4]. Or if again any, as it is affirmed, have been induced to embrace Christianity by the same persuasive agency, we could scarcely boast of those as adding much strength to our religion, who can reject all the historic testimony in support of Christianity, and be convinced of the existence and divinity of Christ by sundry mysterious rappings which convey no intelligible sound, and to which an arbitrary meaning is assigned. He can have given little, if any, serious attention to the evidences of Christianity, who accepts the testimony of one man rather than that of the whole Christian world, and allows the assurances of a "medium,"

---

[4] Brown's "Philosophy of the Mind," Lecture xvii.

who cannot give ocular proof of the spirit's presence, to have greater weight with his reason and judgment than evidences which we can test and examine for ourselves.

No, my brethren. The whole idea and theory of Spiritualism, so far at least as it is at present developed, does violence to notions founded on fact and experience. " The whole extent of our knowledge or imagination reaches not beyond our own ideas, limited to our ways of perception [5]." This fact alone should make us hesitate to accept, as even probable, that which is not within the compass of our understanding. If Spiritualism be but in its infancy we can scarcely hope for a more fruitful and better manhood. It holds out but little promise of this. We have no power to summon and recall the dead. With what new powers and faculties the soul may be invested, we know not. We can only judge of this by our present knowledge. There is a designed and studied reserve maintained throughout Scripture concerning the future state; a reserve which Lazarus did not break, nor the saints which rose at Christ's crucifixion. To evoke the dead for purposes so

[5] Locke, "Essay on the Human Understanding." Book III. ch. xi. sec. 23.

unmeaning and trifling, so aimless and profit-
less, is derogatory if not profane. To believe
that the spirit of one we loved and fondly
cherished will readily obey the summons of
some adventurer, and conspire to assist him in
gaining a livelihood by trading on the feelings,
and taking advantage of the natural inquisi-
tiveness of our nature, is a thought unholy; it
is monstrous in the extreme. If the Romanist
takes advantage of these same feelings to construct an elaborate system of invocation of
saints, masses for the dead, prayers to the departed, and we deem him superstitious, we encourage often a credulity which the Romanist
discountenances, not less fraught with evil, and
not one whit less superstitious.

More rational, more true to our instincts,
more Scriptural is the teaching of our reformed
Church in this matter. The souls of the departed, when they quit this outward material
frame, pass into a state of rest until the consummation of all things. Theirs is the deep
quietness of innermost communion with God.
It is a state of painless expectation, of blissful,
perfect repose. It is blessedness, but not
glory. Death is changed into sleep and the
dead sleep in Jesus. We call our burial

grounds "cemeteries," the Greek word for sleeping-places. "Death is but the prelude—a transitory state, ushering in a mightier power of life. It is a kindly soothing rest to the wearied and world-worn spirit. The grave is little more than the longest night's sleep in the life of an undying soul. The unclothed, disembodied spirit is beyond the affections of decay. There is no weakness, nor weariness. It is rest from labour, rest from warfare against sin; against all its strength, and subtleties, and cares. Satan can tempt no more; the world cannot lure; self cannot betray. There is no more inward struggle; no sliding back again; no swerving aside; no danger of falling. They have gained "the shore of eternal peace." They who are gone before us, in the long history of ages past, await our coming. They await the change that awaits us. Without us they shall not be made perfect, and

> "*Far better they should sleep awhile*
> *Within the Church's shade,*
> *Nor wake, until new heaven, new earth,*
> *Meet for their new immortal birth*
> *For their abiding-place be made,*

> *Than wander back to life, and lean*
> *On our frail love once more* [6].

The living are united with the dead by
many links of union. By a common faith,
by common hopes, by fellowship in the mys-
tical body of Christ our Lord. The unity of
the saints on earth with the Church unseen
is the closest bond of all. It is high, mysterious, holy fellowship. They are not severed,
they are only out of sight. In commemorating the departed we propose to ourselves
examples for our imitation, not objects of
worship. In recognizing departed worth we
do not adore the saint, but the grace of Christ
which made him such. We praise God's holy
name for all His servants departed this life in
His faith and fear. We commend them to
His keeping in the prayer read over the open
grave, "that we, with all those that are
departed in the true faith of Thy holy name,
may have our perfect consummation and bliss,
both in body and soul, in Thy eternal and
everlasting glory." When we think of those
who are gone before us, as think of them we
often and often will, there is one thought, more

"Christian Year"—Burial of the Dead.

practical, more edifying, more consoling, more
Scriptural than the foolish speculations of the
spiritualist. It is a thought which briefly
sums up all that we can, or need concern ourselves to know respecting the departed. It is
implied in my text—

"The memory of the just is blessed."

> "*A sea before*
> *The Throne is spread ; its pure, still glass*
> *Pictures all earth scenes as they pass,*
> *We, on its shore*
> *Share in the bosom of our rest—*
> *God's knowledge, and are blest*[1] *!*"

There is a pious, natural, and legitimate
contemplation of the dead, which for many
reasons should be encouraged. There are few
here, if any, who have not, at some period in
their lives, sustained the loss of a relative or
friend. Many circumstances will serve to
remind us of our loss. The most trifling incident will recall to our memory the object of
our affection. Revisiting the scene or neigh-
bourhood of their former residence—a chance
remark—a familiar tune—similarity of feature

---

[1] " Lyra Apostolica." " Saints Departed."

in others—the lock of hair—the portrait, any of these serves to revive and awaken recollections of a vivid and mournful character. Death itself cannot kill the affection of many years. Separation cannot weaken the tie which binds soul to soul by many sympathies. Affection, love, respect bear down all the barriers and impediments of theology. Sorrow of heart is the best expositor of God's teaching about the departed. Our feelings under bereavement betray the instincts of mankind. The belief of a future recognition and reunion, which Christianity encourages us to expect, is of the nature of an intuition.

It not unfrequently however occurs that the memory of the dead is lost in the stir and throng of active life. Some few will cling to it fondly and tenaciously. Life with all its duties, interests and occupations, has lost its charm with their loss. Everywhere they miss the presence—the voice—the counsel—the love of the companion of years. But, with the vast majority, the unseen world is seldom or never realized. If we have credulity as one extreme we have Sadduceism as the other. The time between death and resurrection is virtually lost sight of. We take but little account of it. We rarely entertain in our minds the fact of an intermediate state. We give few thoughts to the dead. We scarce can bring ourselves to believe that they can have any interest for us now that they have been removed from the midst of us. Life in its varied activity is ever before the eye and presented to our contemplation. Man is seen in his vast assemblage. " Like the evergreens which lose their leaves by individuals and still maintain their living foliage, the human race is, to the thoughtless spectator, presented under such a fallacious appearance, as if it always lived[1]."

Hence the dead are not missed in the crowd and throng of life. When the funeral service is ended, and the last sad offices performed, we are wont to bid a long farewell to him or her whom we have followed to the grave. We anticipate the Resurrection; we virtually overpass in thought the interval which must elapse ere the Resurrection come to pass.

Our Church protests against this by a formal and annual celebration of the memory of the dead. The Festival of All Saints has reference

[1] Foster. Lecture xlvii. "The Autumn and its Moral Analogies."

to the intermediate state. The dead have a real interest for us, though we see and hear them no more. The natural affections which survive their departure are susceptible of being diverted into a profitable channel. Our thoughts under sorrow may take an edifying direction. Though we may not think of those who are gone as having any power to further our salvation by their prayers and intercession, we may contemplate their virtues by way of imitation and example. We may think of their faith, their holiness of life, their consistency of conduct. We may call to mind with profit all the happier traits of their character. We may dwell on those qualities of disposition, and those spiritual graces, which faintly reflected in them the mind of Christ. We may recall the virtues for which in their lifetime they were eminent, the good they strove to do, the pattern they set in the various relationships of life, the spirit in which they performed their duties, the piety and zeal which characterized all their actions, thoughts, and conversation. We may remember how they died—with what calmness and resignation and hope they entered into the valley of the shadow of death, with what peace of mind! The memory of the just embraces the saints of God in all past times. "We are compassed with a great cloud of witnesses." Patriarchs, Prophets, Apostles, the most eminent and zealous promoters of truth and religion in all ages, martyrs, reformers, missionaries, philanthropists, an illustrious shining host, who have bequeathed to posterity a deathless name and high example, these are reckoned with the "just."

This is the more general and comprehensive interpretation of the text. We realize the value of departed worth more strongly and vividly as it comes nearer home to our own individual experience, as we remember it in many who have entered into their rest; in the instances of a parent who watched us in infancy and instructed us in youth—in the case of any who have ever been bound to us by the closest ties, and associated in our memory with the fondest recollections.

Doubtless, with yourselves, my brethren, there have been known to you amongst your acquaintance, and in the more private circle of home life, some, who though they are gone yet remain unalterably fixed and cherished in your memory in this distinct character of "the just." You could mention by name one or more who abide in the picture-gallery of the mind, and ever will, as long as you live, kept alive there as the images, the examples, the personifications of what we instinctively approve, admire, and feel that we ought to love and be. Such memories as these, which bring to the eye the gushing tear, may have, if rightly used, a very salutary effect upon the mind. They may even operate as a motive with some, added to all other and higher motives, to lead a Christian life. Imagination peoples space with departed kinsmen and friends. We find consolation in the thought that they are near and about us. This may be true to reality or not. It may be no more than poetry and sentiment. They may be endowed with faculties of vision, by which they see and notice us, we all the while, because of the screen which hides them from our view, being unconscious of their presence. It may be they know all our history, our sins, our failures, our better efforts, our success. We cannot tell. We may however recall their memory. We may reflect how it would grieve one dear to memory, who was ever solicitous for our spiritual welfare, did he see us about to commit some wilful sin, or yielding to some temptation. And that thought—even that thought—may make us retrace our erring steps. It may bring back to our mind that last affecting scene,—that death-bed exhortation,—so as to unnerve and shame us. It may keep us from the sin, and the scenes of sin, which we were about to enter. It may quell the rising passion. It may restrain us, through a misgiving which haunts us, lest any we loved too well to grieve, should see our fall, our broken faith, our sad infirmity.

In our efforts after a life of holiness we may think how it would add to their saintly bliss could they but see our efforts. For it may be they know all now. If they have not perfect fruition they have at least a foretaste, and this knowledge would enhance the good they might see in us. They could foresee to what, if persevered in, it must inevitably lead. Added then to all other and higher motives to perseverance there is this, when we think of our Christian friends departed this life, that their deepest sympathies are awakened for us. That as we grow holier, we grow nearer to them, and make more sure that future reunion which nothing again may interrupt or sever.

Surely then we may say that " the memory of the just is blessed," if only their example provokes our imitation, and their influence is still felt for good. Surely their memory is blessed, if

the young are restrained from vice and checked
in the commission of sin, by hearing once more,
as it were, the voice of dying parents, as with
failing breath and faltering tongue they com-
mended their child to the keeping of God, and
prayed that His fear and grace might rest upon
him. We may bless God for His saints departed
this life, if one in the vigour of manhood or of
womanhood, or it may be more advanced still,—
one on whom the snows of winter have fallen,—
can look back on some scene of earlier days, and
feel that even now, notwithstanding that the
former freshness of feeling is gone, and the
mind, from constant contact with the world, is
less open to impression,—that even now, the
memory of that scene has a power and an unweakened influence, bringing, it may be, tears
to the eye that but seldom weeps, kindling
emotions now but rarely felt, awakening fresh
impulses towards a better life.

Thoughts such as these are legitimate. They
do not trespass on forbidden ground. They
accord with our innermost feelings. They are
not unprofitable. Their memory is blessed who
illustrate God's grace in the soul. Their
memory is blessed to whom the mind reverts as
practical proofs of the excellence of genuine

religion. Their memory is blessed who lived in the fear of God, who died reposing entirely on the finished work of Christ, and yielded up their spirits in perfect trust. This is a memory which promotes the sense of a social relation with the state beyond the grave. This is the medium, the bond which serves to keep up an intercourse between the living and the dead. And the pious mind, free alike from superstition and credulity, knowing that there can be no sensible intercommunication, can through a contemplative faith almost already realize that happier state " where the wicked cease from troubling and the weary are at rest."

Seek not then, my Christian brethren, to recall the dead, rather recall the virtues which endear them to your memory. Encourage not a credulity which borders on blasphemy. Live rather in constant remembrance of those graces of character which make us meet for the inheritance of the saints in light. Vex not yourselves with surmisings as to the actual whereabouts and conditions of the spirit world; rather concern yourselves with thoughts of greater moment, even your own spiritual state—your preparation for Eternity. Discountenance, as much as lies in your power, that morbid curiosity

concerning the dead which brings no blessing
with it. Encourage the piety which will make
your death a change to be desired—the birthday
of the soul's eternal bliss. Seek the Holy Spirit
of God, that you may enjoy the felicity of His
chosen people. Pray that you may be sanctified
in Christ Jesus. Get rid of that sin, whatever
it may be, which hinders now your communion
with God, and which, if unrepented of and not
forsaken, will shut the gates of Paradise against
you. Recognize the limits which Divine wisdom
has seen fit to prescribe. Let nothing tempt
you to trespass these; and if at any time
your aching, sorrow-stricken heart should, under
the afflictive dispensation of Providence, lead you,
almost against your will, to desire some more
certain knowledge concerning those you love,
stay and comfort your troubled spirit by passages
such as these, full of consolation :—

"Right dear in the sight of the Lord is the
death of His saints [9]."   .

Again : "I would not have you ignorant concerning them which are asleep, that ye sorrow
not even as others which have no hope. For if
we believe that Jesus died and rose again, even

[9] Ps. cxvi. 13.

so them also which sleep in Jesus will God bring with Him [1]."

Once more : "These are they which came out of great tribulation, and have washed their robes and made them white in the blood of the Lamb.

" Therefore are they before the throne of God, and serve Him day and night in His temple : and He that sitteth on the throne shall dwell among them.

" They shall hunger no more, neither thirst any more ; neither shall the sun light on them, nor any heat.

" For the Lamb, which is in the midst of the throne shall feed them, and shall lead them unto living fountains of waters ; and God shall wipe away all tears from their eyes [2]."

There is yet one other reflection which this subject suggests, one which it will not need many words to enforce. As year by year we commemorate the dead and the memory of the just, remember—remember that you too must die. You yourself must join the spirit world. Wherever that world may be, your soul must pass into it hence. Ere many years shall have passed, you

---

[1] 1 Thess. iv. 13, 14. [2] Rev. vii. 14—17.

K

and I will be of those of whom men shall speak
as "the departed." Much around us serves to
remind us of our end. The falling leaves of
this Autumn season, which we tread under our
feet, are Nature's silent yet eloquent testimony.
Remember that to leave behind us when we die a
memory which others shall bless, is better than
transient worldly fame—more enduring than any
other fleeting reputation—more to be desired
than mines of wealth stored up for another's use.
This is not a passion for vain glory—it is a
praiseworthy desire that the remembrance which
will remain and linger in the minds of those
who survive us, should not be one causing pain,
disappointment, bitterness, or shame. A wish to
be, in remembrance, numbered with the faithful
and zealous servants of God and Christ. A wish
to leave our names and memory so associated
with all that is good, that men may say of us,
"Though dead he yet speaketh." A wish to
remain, as long as remembered, a motive, an
argument, and incitement to all good to those
who follow. Thus to be doing good long after
we shall have gone hence, when our voice is
hushed in the unbroken stillness of the grave,
and the place know us no more.

Go your ways from this house, my brethren,

in which we have together dwelt on this solemn theme, carrying with you into your daily life reflections such as these. Live by God's gracious help as He would have you do, as all who most loved you could desire, as you will wish you had done, when you come to lay yourself down for the last time on that bed of sickness from which you shall be borne with solemn steps to the grave. So that in years and years to come, when all trace of you shall have vanished, your good example shall be blessed to the souls of many; that when Christians meet, as we have met, to commemorate the departed, we may be numbered with Christ's elect, this being the brief record and epitome of your life :

"The memory of the just is blessed."

SERMON VI.

THE REMEMBRANCE OF SIN[1].

DEUT. ix. 22.

" At Taberah, and at Massah, and at Kibroth-hataavah, ye provoked the Lord to wrath."

THE greater portion of the Book of Deuteronomy, as the title implies, is a repetition of the Mosaic law, or a review of the people of Israel. Moses, himself now full of years, admonishes the Israelites as they were nearing that promised land, a distant prospect of which he was given to view from Mount Pisgah, but into which he himself was not permitted to enter. His admonition has the more force and weight, inasmuch as he had accompanied the Israelites throughout all their pilgrimage of forty years.

---

[1] Preached on The Second Sunday in Lent.

Forty years in which some who were prattling children when they first entered on it, had grown up around him into manhood and womanhood; some who were in the prime of life at its commencement, were now greyhaired and in the sunset of their days; some of the more aged had fallen asleep in the wilderness. His own days were numbered; a peculiar solemnity attaches itself therefore to his exhortations, spoken as they were in view of his approaching end. Before he takes a long leave of those who had grown up around him from their childhood, over whom, amidst many provocations, he had watched with more than a fatherly tenderness, and guided through all the intricacies of the desert, he summons them together in the plains of Moab. Ere long he must bid them farewell. All the yearnings of his heart towards those whose fortunes he had shared compel him to admonish them for the future by the recollection of the past. He bids them over and over again to take a mental pilgrimage over all the track which they had travelled in the course of that forty years, and to connect such a review of their past life with beneficial uses which might influence for good their future lives.

No one reading these exhortations can fail to

be struck with the frequency of these appeals to
the past, with the enunciation of specific, particular sins and transgressions of which the Israelites had already been guilty. Moses mentions
separately, in detail, and one by one, particular occasions, particular times, particular places
where they had been rebellious, had grievously
sinned, and had incurred the wrath and vengeance
of an offended God. *" Remember and forget not.
Remember and forget not."* It is thus he emphatically warns them, not by the prediction of
possible dangers, looking with the eye of a seer
into the dim and misty future, but by the confessed experience of the past; by that knowledge
of the character of the Israelites which the
experience of forty years had given him, and
which throughout that whole period had been
uniformly of a rebellious type. As they stood
around him, young and old, children and
parents, he reminded them and called on them
to remember for themselves some few of the
more remarkable occasions on which they had
erred. At *Taberah*[2], where they murmured
against God, distrusted His providential care,
and where many of their number were con-

---

[2] Numb. xi. 1—4.

sumed. At *Massah* [3], where " they tempted the Lord, saying, Is the Lord amongst us or not ? " Again at *Kibroth-hataavah* [4], where they lusted after evil things—that spot in the desert known and designated as *" sepulchra concupiscentiæ,"* *the graves of lust.*

There was much wisdom shown in thus reminding the Israelites of the past. As hitherto rebellion against God had been their characteristic, besetting sin, so—judging from the force of habit—it was most likely still to be. This was the danger he foresaw for them in their future, founded on what he already knew of them, and they knew of themselves. Their sin lay in one particular direction. As hitherto it had invariably drawn down vengeance upon them, so they might feel sure it would always do. When they looked back, therefore, on the past, these places would serve as landmarks recording the occasions, the scenes, the circumstances of sin. And this review, this recollection was to be turned by them to good account. When the mind reverted to the past, the painful recollection was to operate with salutary effect as a warning for the future. It

---

[3] Exod. xvii. 7. [4] Numb. xi. 34.

should inspire fear and suggest caution. It should humble them in their own eyes. The recollection of God's forbearance, rather than lead to or encourage presumption, should make them doubly jealous of again grieving Him by a recurrence to any former sin. With a view, therefore, to their future good, Moses thus reminds the Israelites in the detailed recapitulation of my text—

"*At Taberah, and at Massah, and at Kibroth-hataavah, ye provoked the Lord to wrath.*"

During this solemn season, brethren, there is one subject to which especial prominence is given, and on which you are frequently exhorted to meditate with seriousness, and that is Sin— Sin, which was the cause of the humiliation of our blessed Redeemer, and of His atoning sacrifice on the Cross of Calvary. And plainly something more is necessary, if our meditation is to lead to any practical result, than that we should merely think of Sin as a bad element in the moral world, as the fruitful cause of all the disharmony in the universe, as a mysterious blight that has settled on a fair Creation. All this is very true of Sin, but thoughts such as these which are taken up with the mystery and nature, and origin, and theory of Sin will lead

to very little or no practical good. Reflections
of this nature are external to ourselves, they do
not affect the conscience. It is on our own individual sinfulness in the sight of God that we are
to meditate. We are to be personally humbled
at the thought of our own and manifold transgressions. Our own shortcomings and negli-
gences, our own wilful and presumptuous sins
in times past, our present evil tendencies and
sinful habits; these are what we are now to
think of, and to ponder over, and lament, if we
would have the forgiveness of Christ. True and
sincere repentance there cannot be with any
one of us, unless there be this meditation on
self, this self-accusing, self-chiding spirit. Mere
general, liturgical confessions of sinfulness do
not bring with them that humbling, saddening, salutary sorrow which this retrospection,
this mental turning of the eye on ourselves, if
accompanied with prayer, cannot fail to produce. Nor will it be necessary here to remark
that such repentance must be not only real and
sincere, but also that it must needs be a conscious, spiritual exercise of the mind, a matter
of inward feeling. If we would know what our
real spiritual condition is, we must be very
candid with ourselves. We must from time to

time review our past life. We must recall the
sins of childhood or youth which are the pro-
jected shadows of the sins of more mature years.
We must go over the ground again of years that
are fled and gone, because those past years are
not unimportant. They have contributed to the
formation of our present character, whatever
that may be, just as surely as we have grown up
from our earliest infancy, retaining still in our
manhood or old age certain physical features
which serve to establish the identity of our physical nature throughout each progressive stage
of existence. Does not the river flowing in its
broader current and deeper channel bear along
with it the waters of the lesser stream which
gave it birth? Does not the sturdy oak of a
century's growth retain the characteristics of
the sapling out of which it has gradually
grown? Surely this is so. For all real
and practical self-examination, then, the retrospect and review 'of life must have a prominent place assigned to it. Reflection must form
a very essential element of repentance. Why so?
Because we are apt to live in the Present. Present actions, present occupations—these absorb
our attention. Yesterday, with all its circumstances, unless of a very marked character,

quickly passes out of sight. It fades from the memory like the shifting scenes in the moving panorama which give place to other and new. And it is so with our sins. One hides the other, slips behind it and out of sight; is forgotten in the temptations and transgressions of another day. All that is past is in a certain sense dead. It is buried in the sepulchre of departed years. We mourn over the Present, but we rarely mourn over that Past which was once ours as surely as the Present now is, and which has helped to make us what we now are.

It is true that the surrounding circumstances of that past life cannot be rearranged; the external accidents cannot be put together again in the same form and shape, under the same conditions of time and place as before. But though these have vanished, the spirit of our existence as well as the fact of that existence remains. Human life is not a series of abrupt transitions. We do not step with a bound over any chasm which divides childhood from infancy, manhood from both, old age from all. Our life is one unbroken, uninterrupted chain of existence from the cradle to the grave, each period colouring that which succeeds it with its own hue. Infancy tinges childhood; childhood gives youth its proper complexion; youth fixes these colours in manhood; manhood retains the deeper dye in old age. And so the sins of past years, even though we rarely think of them, while they have been characteristic of us as the outward development and working of particular sinful inclinations, prompted and acted upon by outward congenial temptations, are the sins which will most probably be ours to the very end of our days, unless overcome within us by the grace of God aiding our own individual efforts after holiness.

This it is that makes the sin of our earlier life so important; it will follow us throughout our life. It will cleave and cling closely to us if encouraged and indulged, growing upon us with our growth, intertwining itself, like the ivy parasite, in the root and stem and branch of our nature, or like the [5] Murderer tree of the Brazilian forest, which growing side by side with the tender sapling, at last overtops it and kills it in its fatal folds. Because we have once in years past fallen into sin, that sin has become ours,

[5] Bates. "Naturalist on the Amazons."

and we are therefore never secure against falling into it again. It has henceforth become associated, identified with us. It is our besetting sin, indulged in in youth and ever ready to betray us again. Hence it is also that every man's life, however outwardly uneventful, is full of importance the very moment he looks back upon it, for it becomes to him a connected history; each period interwoven with the last, sending its influence onward into it, determining and shaping his individual character. Thus by reflection, he sees it in its true light, in its relation, as a whole, to eternity. And all along those past years there is the Taberah and the Massah, and the Kibroth-hataavah of some day or hour or season of special sin. Is not this true of us all?

God has endowed us with a very wonderful power of the mind. It is that power or faculty which in its reflex exercise and operation is known as memory. It is this power of the mind which gives life once more to the past. It revives in the mind long-forgotten scenes. It conjures up before our mental vision departed days and years, if not in all their detailed circumstances, yet in their imperishable spirit. But for memory how much of our former life would scarcely ever be realized! Through this faculty we are enabled to condense successive and distant periods of time into one. We can extract their essence, as we extract the perfume and fragrance from fallen leaves. Thus we speak of our childhood as thoughtless, passionate, or frivolous; of our youth as indolent and misspent. We can recall at will certain seasons of repentance or occasions of wilful sin; and although, as I have already said, all the surrounding circumstances of a particular sin may no longer exist, yet it has left an indelible impression on the mind, as the scar remains imprinted on the outward features, as the sandstone retains in fossil the mark of the raindrop where it fell, as the tree wears engraved on its bark the trace of the injury it once received.

There are very few who, as they look back upon their past life, cannot put their finger down, as it were, on the fact of past sins. We remember what we did in childhood that was wrong. We remember how we grieved God's Spirit in advancing years. We can recall some planned, deliberate, self-chosen sin. We know *where* it was committed. We know *when* it was committed. We know *how* it was committed. This, too, over and above those minor faults which led up to the wilful sin, such as remissness in devotional exercises; harbouring sinful thoughts in our mind without any effort to dislodge and expel them; indulging in a long train of sinful imaginations; not watching against the increasing worldliness of spirit which was growing upon us, and that general lowering of the tone of our religious life which prepares us naturally for the climax of some one act of impurity, dishonesty, tempting of Providence, and forgetfulness of Him. Though years may have gone by, and our present life be amidst new and different scenes, still we can never *forget* the occasion of some past sin, still less the swift judgment which overtook us, or the merciful forbearance which spared us. It never was intended that we should forget these passages in our life. The mind has this wonderful power of retaining impressions, especially if they be of a marked character. This is true, not only in connexion with particular good or noble actions, but it is a matter of familiar experience in other respects also. The Naturalist, for example, speaks of the indelible impression which certain incidents in his communion with Nature have made and left on his mind, impressed there with a vividness which he feels will never be effaced, and all the more observable from the ever-increasing dimness and vagueness into which the contemporary impressions are fading. The nocturnal utterances of a particular bird, which he had ardently desired to hear; the vivid emotion of delight excited on finding a beautiful spemen of some rare object; the solemn grandeur of a primæval forest, with a subdued light penetrating the massive foliage, like that which, passing through a stained glass window, is diffused throughout the cathedral pile; the first sight of some magnificent water-lily, these are epochs in the life of the Naturalist,—landmarks standing out like the promontory of some long line of coast, bold and clear, though the intervening shore is lost to view. Can we not well understand how the great traveller in the interior of Africa, could never look in after years on a spray of the forked moss without having the scene of his despondency brought vividly before his mind, without recalling the hour when, weary and exhausted, he had laid him down in the lonely desert to die, parched with fever heat, despairing of life? His eye chanced to light on the tiny moss. He reflected that the same Divine Being who made that slender plant to grow and thrive beneath the rays of the scorching sun, would watch with loving care and protection over him. The thought inspired him with new hope and courage. Could the remembrance of that day ever pass and fade away [6] ?

And can the memory of particular days in our own life ever pass away? Can we think of them as having no longer any interest for us, as fraught with no remaining consequence? Have we no landmarks here and there, marking out certain spots in our past history, which we should do well to remember? Have not some scenes, some actions, some transgressions more than others left their impression which nothing can efface, burnt in, branded, as it were, upon the memory? Cannot each one of us readily recall circumstances which passed so rapidly as almost to have been unnoticed at the time, but which were in reality stamping upon our hearts an impress which was to last for ever and for ever,—particular occasions of sin which are still remembered whilst whole portions of our lives are forgotten—because we find in them the

---

[6] " Romance of Natural History." (Gosse.)

L

germs of our present character. These still live
because they affected that spiritual nature which
is itself immortal. They helped to form in us
settled habits. May not we in part apply to
ourselves the solemn admonition of the law-
giver of old :—" At Taberah, and at Massah, at
Kibroth-hataavah, ye provoked the Lord to
wrath."

Speaking now, as I trust I am, to many
amongst you here, if not all, who are earnest
and sincere in your intention of using this season of self-recollection aright; to such of you as
conscientiously and prayerfully examine yourselves ; who do not intend to allow these few
weeks of more than usual solemnity to come to a
close without your having extracted some spiritual good from them, be it greater knowledge of
self, deeper conviction of personal sinfulness,
lower degrees of humiliation, a more awakened
sense of the necessity of Christ's Atonement;
who have formed resolutions for the future, be
it greater watchfulness against particular sins,
stricter devotion, more real self-denial ; speaking
to such here, let me remind you that in connexion with your self-examination, memory,
memory may be a very great help to you. To
dwell upon distinct, separate, well-known, and

remembered occasions of past sinfulness may operate with salutary effect. This reflection may be turned, as God would have us turn it, to good and beneficial uses. It is fraught with danger if we do not use it wisely and aright.

Consider for a moment. Sin from its very nature can never be otherwise than hateful and abominable in God's sight. This it ought to be in our own. Whenever we have sinned we have lost so much innocence, so much purity. We are not what we might have been had we not sinned. To touch sin is to be defiled by contact with it. To have fallen under its power is to have fallen from grace.

Therefore to remember past sins without unfeigned sorrow is only to sin over again—is only to sin over again. To use this faculty of Memory for the purpose of going over mentally the particulars of some former transgression, with a secret hankering after it, can only be full of peril. To retraverse the journey of our life, particular stages of which are connected with humbling recollections, and yet not to be saddened as we halt at these stages, only too clearly indicates that we have never yet sincerely repented of the past. This is to look back like Lot's wife. This is to be like the sailor, to throw overboard the ship's cargo in a storm and to wish for it again in a calm.

God alone can look on evil without contamination. "Memory," as it has been well said, "like a river, is tinged with the soil through which it winds its sullen way." The recollection of our sins is only safe when it forms part of our self-reproaching, part of our self-humiliation. It is unsafe, most unsafe, if we excuse the sin, when we remember it, as only the infirmity of our time of life, and think lightly and leniently of it. It is unsafe, most unsafe, if it does not excite in us a salutary fear of offending in like manner again, a lively sense of God's forbearance in giving us more time for repentance, and, with the Syrophenician woman of whom we have this day read [7], the importunate cry for the mercy of Christ. Memory then is only abused, that is to say, it is not turned to good account when it does not lead to and produce such results as these.

On the other hand, Memory may be a great help to us. If, as we review our life and recall the pollutions that have stained it, our forgetfulness of God in prosperity, our murmurings

---

[7] Gospel for the Second Sunday in Lent.

under some afflicting dispensation, temptation
yielded to, resolutions unfulfilled, the vow such as
that of Baptism or Confirmation broken, duties
neglected, sinful tempers betrayed; if, as we
dwell on these separately, not only a livelier
sense of guilt is awakened in us, and the thought
of Christ, by Whose atoning blood our sinful
souls are cleansed, is made more precious to us,
but if this review makes us more cautious, more
guarded, more circumspect for the future, in such
case Memory is turned to good account. For
we are not in remembering past sin to linger
over it. We are not to waste time in fruitless
regrets. The sin has been done, and now
nothing can undo it. No amount of repentance, of zeal, of self-denial, can restore to us the
innocence we have once lost. As well might we,
who are thus far advanced in life, hope to retrace our steps and return to our purer childhood again. No. This cannot be. But as past
sins indicated our particular character, and as
what we have already done amiss serves not only
to reveal to us our characteristic weakness but
also, through the very force and law of habit,
shows us in what and where our danger still
lies, the review of the past should lead to the

distinct practical result of inspiring us with salutary fear for the future. As we look back shuddering at the thought of some imminent danger from which as by a narrow hair-breadth we escaped; as the sailor gives a wide berth to the reef on which he has once been wrecked, so ought we to determine in our minds that we will for the future—so long as our lives are still spared—avoid the occasion of a sin to which we once yielded; that we will henceforth shun the scenes and surrounding circumstances which might revive its power; that we will pray God, for Christ's sake, for His Spirit to work in us that one particular grace of which the knowledge of our past weakness and present infirmity reminds us we most stand in need; that we will seek more humbly, more earnestly, more *importunately*, for the grace of Christ in our hearts to keep us from falling.

This is to turn our past and sorrowful experience, brethren, to good account. This is to carry with us into our future years, be they many or few, such a remembrance of our provocations and of God's mercies as shall give increased earnestness to that great work, the salvation of the undying soul; a work which ought never to be carried on in a careless, lukewarm, luxurious, indolent spirit, when such momentous issues as life and death are at stake. God requires of each one of us here, not only a remembrance of the Past, but amendment for the Future.

Live, we say to you, with this thought ever present to your mind, that to-morrow and to-day will have become yesterday, with its record of good and evil, with its own history all bearing on your future destiny and existence. Confront your yesterdays with penitence and with prayer. Hide not from yourself the full importance of the Past. Disguise not from yourself its real relation to the Present, its intimate connexion with the Future. Now in the day of grace and opportunity; now ere the door be shut and closed, and we knock only in vain; now in this, "the accepted time," when the powers of mind are still yours and its faculties in full vigour; now when you can fold your hands in prayer, and your tongue is not yet silent in the grave; when the soul, sin-stained, burdened with many a painful recollection, can yet turn to the Cross of Christ and with the eye of faith can look on Him, the Healer of our souls, let not these opportunities pass away unimproved.

We need not to confess our fault,
  For surely Thou canst tell,
What we have done and what we are,
  Thou, O God, knowest well.
Therefore to beg and to entreat,
  With tears we come to Thee ;
As children that have done amiss
  Fall at their Father's knee.

And need we then, O Lord, repeat
  The blessing which we crave ;
When Thou dost know before we speak
  The thing that we would have ?
Mercy, O Lord, mercy we ask,
  This is the total sum.
For mercy, Lord, is all our prayer ;
  O ! Let thy mercy come.   Amen.

SERMON VII.

THE DANGER OF RELAPSE.

LUKE xi. 24—26.

" *When the unclean spirit is gone out of a man,*
he walketh through dry places, seeking rest;
and finding none, he saith, I will return into
my house whence I came out.
" *And when he cometh, he findeth it swept and*
garnished. Then goeth he, and taketh to him
seven other spirits more wicked than himself;
and they enter in, and dwell there: and the
last state of that man is worse than the first [1].*"

THE immediate occasion of these words was the
casting out a devil. The fact was so confessed
that the people accepted it as a sign of what it
really was, viz., the supernatural power of
Christ and a proof of His mission. The
Pharisees, unable to deny the fact and equally

[1] Gospel for the Third Sunday in Lent.

unable to attribute it to any known natural
agency, ascribed the miracle to the effect of that
evil magic, a belief in which still propagated
itself among the traditions of Jewish fanaticism.
Our Lord replies to this accusation by showing
how inconsistent it was with the very idea of
evil. It carried with it its own refutation.
For it was a contradiction in terms to suppose
that any one should be freed *from* the power
of the Evil One *by* the power of the Evil
One. "If Satan also be divided against himself, how shall his kingdom stand?" He ex-
pressly and emphatically affirms that the devil
was cast out "with the finger of God," i. e.,
that a higher power than Satan was developed
in the world—a supernatural power which He
had himself just exercised, superior and in direct
opposition to the power of Satan. All other,
even apparent cures of demoniacs wrought on any
other principle than this could only be apparent
and deceptive. They treated the *symptoms*, and
the symptoms only. They did not reach the
radical cause of the possession. The Jewish
exorcists, therefore, even supposing that any
results followed from their professed magic and
incantation, or from any influence which they
may have powerfully exercised over the ima-

gination of the patient, could never perform a radical cure, because, however temporarily thwarted or restrained, the dominion of the evil principle remained really unshaken and unweakened. The very agency which removed the symptoms for a time would only strengthen the cause of these outward symptoms, to break forth again with increased power. Therefore, Christ not only does not recognize any cure as genuine which is not wrought by the power of the Spirit of God—and this is what is meant when He says, " He that is not with Me is against Me "—but more than this, unless the cure of the demoniac is effected by the redeeming power of the Divine Spirit, the apparently cured disease breaks out again with renewed force; the ungodly spirit returns to its old haunts; " the last state of that man is worse than the first."

The whole subject of demoniacal possession, such as that described and recorded in the New Testament, is of necessity involved in much mystery. That it should be so will be the more readily understood when we remember that like the gift of tongues, demoniacal possession has ceased to exist. If it still survive it is no longer manifested in the same visible manner, nor is it accompanied with the

same physical characteristics and conditions[2].
That it was a distinct psychical disease, is evident
from the fact that it is clearly distinguished in
Scripture from epilepsy, melancholy, and mere
insanity.   The Evangelists classify demoniacal
possession apart from diseases[3].   Exorcism and
exorcists were recognized in the early Church
as concerned with a special form and manifestation of Satanic influence.   Our Lord uniformly
speaks of demoniacs as persons not merely of disordered intellect, but as beings retaining the
distinct consciousness of their own individuality.
Ever and anon fitful gleams of their better
nature broke forth, but they were under the
thraldom and mastery of an alien spiritual might.
Christ invariably addresses the spirit as distinct
from the man.   He uses language which was
not merely in conformity with Jewish notions,
but which would have been inconsistent with
the actual phenomena recorded, if we are to consider these cases of demoniacs as nothing more
than bodily ailments.   The Jews themselves,
whilst they rightly attributed all human diseases
or bodily defects to sin, and directly to Satan,
did not regard all persons afflicted with sickness

---

[2] Trench on the Miracles.
[3] Matt. iv. 24; viii. 16.   Mark i. 34.

as *demoniacs.* There seems, in fact, to be little doubt that there were certain features, broadly marked, which served at once to distinguish one "possessed" from one suffering from physical disease. And it is important, in endeavouring to conceive what these features could have been, to observe that our Lord on all occasions seeks to impress on the minds of those who witnessed these cures, the existence, the separate existence, the reality of a fallen, apostate spirit. He insists on the personality of Satan as the fount and source of all that evil in the world, which He came to contend with and to overthrow. Consistently with this truth, He addresses the demoniacs who were not merely great sufferers, but in whom the physical and spiritual were strangely blended. As Archbishop Trench observes, " We find in the demoniac the sense of a misery in which he does not acquiesce ; the deep feeling of inward discord, of the true love utterly shattered, of an alien power which has mastered him wholly, and now is cruelly lording over him, and ever drawing further away from Him in Whom only any created intelligence can find rest and peace '." Hence we find that these

---

' Trench on the Miracles.

demoniacs were the special objects of Christ's healing power. Their sense of misery and yearning for deliverance explains this. That view of the subject seems to have much to recommend it which regards these cases as real possessions by the Evil Spirit. It has been remarked that as the ailments of the body are closely connected with those of the soul, so we find that great plagues have often spread over the earth, coeval with some general crisis in the moral and spiritual world. Neander adduces several instances of this [5]. It has been observed by other writers:—"The predominance of certain spiritual maladies at certain epochs of the world's history which were specially fitted for their generation, with their gradual decline and disappearance in others less congenial, is a fact itself admitting no manner of question [6]." The coming of Christ was just one of these crises. It was an age of spiritual and physical distress, of manifold and violent disruptions. The sway of demonism was a sign of the

[5] E. g. the plague at Athens and the Peloponnesian war; the plagues under the Antonines and Decius; the *tabes inguinaria* at the end of the sixth century, the *ignis sacer* in the eleventh, the *black death* in the fourteenth. (Neander Life of Christ, p. 149.)

[6] Trench, p. 163.

approaching dissolution of the Old World. Its
phenomena were symptoms of the universally
felt discord, the sense of disharmony, the wreck
and confusion of man's spiritual life which pre-
eminently marked the period of our Saviour's
coming, and pointed to it as that which was to
restore harmony and order out of this moral
chaos. We might naturally, therefore, expect
—if there be any truth in the observations made
—to find this same period characterized by the
prevalence of some special malady. And, in
point of fact, we do find a malady to have
prevailed in our Lord's time, which assumed
the form of demoniacal possession. Demoniacal
possession seems to have been an imitation
on the part of Satan of the Incarnation of
Christ. As has been pointed out by Woodward[7] in his essay, " In the conflict which has
been carried on between God and Satan upon the
theatre of this world, the most successful device
which infernal malice could suggest for the
seduction and ruin of mankind has been a perverted imitation of the Divine economy." We
have instances and illustrations of this in Satan's
conversation with Eve in Paradise, in the coun-

[7] See the admirable essay by Woodward on Demoniacal
Possession. (Masters. 1849.)

terfeit of the miracles of Moses by the Egyptian magicians, and of prophetic inspiration by lying spirits and delusive miracles. The worship of the one Living God was turned into innumerable forms of idol worship. Animal sacrifice, the symbolical acknowledgment of the guilt of sin and of the need of an atonement was depraved into the blood-stained offerings of sons and daughters unto devils. The great verities of the mystery of the Trinity were parodied by the fictions of mythology. The Apostles had to contend with " false apostles, deceitful workers, transforming themselves into the apostles of Christ; and no marvel, for Satan himself is transformed into an angel of light [8]." The self-denying precepts of the Gospel were corrupted into "doctrines of devils, forbidding to marry, and commanding to abstain from meats, which God hath created to be received with thanksgiving [9]." And this demoniacal possession is the most striking instance of the Satanic imitation of the Divine economy. It was the diabolical counterfeit of the Incarnation. As the " Word became flesh," and thus new powers of *good* were communicated to man, the Devil

---

[8] 2 Cor. xi. 13, 14.
[9] 1 Tim. iv. 3.

uniting his subject spirits [1] with human spirits
communicated new faculties of *evil.* Such a
physical incorporation of an evil spirit with a
human subject was plainly different from all
previous Satanic operations. We do not read
of such cases prior or subsequent to our Lord's
Ascension. Cotemporary with the coming of
Christ, Satan makes this last effort to imitate
the actions and dispensations of the Supreme.
After the Ascension of our Lord, when Satan's
power was broken and overcome, we do not meet
with cases similar to those possessions with which
our Lord dealt. It is in remarkable confirmation of this that the words δαιμονιζόμενος and
δαιμόνια ἔχειν, which are the words constantly
employed throughout the Four Gospels to
express the seizure of a human subject by an
incarnate demon, are not used in a single instance to describe the agency of Satan subsequent to the Ascension. Upon this point, however, I cannot now enter further than to remark
that the cases of unclean spirits which are met

---

[1] The Devil (ὁ διάβολος). The supreme power of evil is
never spoken of as himself possessing a human subject. The
word usually employed in the New Testament to express the
possessing evil spirit is δαιμόνιον, a term never applied to
Satan.

M

with, subsequent to our Lord's Ascension, all show us that the power of Satan was mutilated and curtailed. If his influence is still apparent, it is exercised in willing subjects, or it is shown in such effects of bodily influence as Satan is still permitted to minister. But the strong one has been overcome by the stronger. It was plainly part. of our Lord's mission that He should overcome Satan in this new region of his dominion. He must bring supernatural power to bear successfully on this new form of supernatural disease; and although, as is very probable, a condition favourable to such "possession" had been superinduced by sensuality, by habitual indulgence in wilful sin, yet He must assert His Divine power, and by removing the fundamental disease of human nature through the operation of His Spirit, restore at the same time its original harmony disturbed by sin [2].

It is most probable, if not almost certain, that possession by an evil spirit, i. e. an actual, physical incorporation of a demon with a human being, is no longer known. So dreadful a union may have been rendered practically impossible by virtue of the Incarnation of our Lord Jesus

[2] See also Barry's article on Demoniacs. Smith's Bible Dict. vol. i. p. 425.

Christ. But the power of Satan, though weakened and broken, is still great. As then, so
now also, this same characteristic of *restlessness*,
of busy activity,—leaving the subject of his
malice for a while, and returning to his old
haunt with sevenfold strength,—is, as human
experience can abundantly testify, still real and
still true.

It was the belief of the Jews that demons
wandered in deserts, in lonely spots uninhabited
by man, in *"dry places* [3]." It is at least a sin-
gular coincidence that our Lord should have
been "led up into the wilderness to be tempted
of the devil." Whether this idea be fanciful or
not, the *restlessness* of Satan, the wandering to
and fro, "seeking rest and finding none," is
strikingly illustrated in the words of my text.
It is thus that Satan is represented in the book
of Job: "The Lord said unto Satan, Whence
comest thou? Then Satan answered the Lord,
and said, From going to and fro in the earth,
and from walking up and down in it [4]." Again,
in the New Testament, St. Peter writes of
Satan in the same terms, "Be sober, be vigi-
lant, because your adversary, the devil, as a

This belief probably grounded on Isaiah xiii. 19—22.
[4] Job i. 7.

M 2

roaring lion, walketh about, seeking whom he may devour[5]."

Few of us fully realize the fact of the existence and activity of the Evil Spirit. We think of Temptation as coming from ourselves and from our own nature. We do not realize it as the direct instigation of the Evil One. Through want of thus realizing the watchful activity of Satan, and from not being habitually on our guard against him, we become in one sense " possessed." This is true of us all, as our own experience confirms, when we review our lives and recall the occasions and circumstances of some wilful sin. As we look back upon some wilful sin, we see how surely it was committed at the instigation of the devil, taking advantage of our unguarded moments, and prompting us to do that which we well knew was wrong, adding the power of his own wickedness to our natural inclinations, and so leading us to commit the sin. This restlessness and activity on the part of Satan, against which our Lord would warn us, is still more vividly realized and understood when we reflect on those *relapses*, on that frequent falling away from grace, which is the

[5] 1 Pet. v. 8.

particular thought of this portion of Scripture.
For herein we read of the expulsion of evil for a
while, and of its return back again with sevenfold strength. Who of us here has not known
these relapses, this falling away from baptismal
grace? Is it not one of the most sad, humili-
ating, and mournful acts in our spiritual life?
Is it not a truth which they who sincerely
examine themselves as to what progress they
are making in grace, have the most often to
mourn over and lament? How often we have
grieved God's Spirit, so that having received It,
It has departed from us, has been withdrawn
from us, leaving us without defence in our sinful weakness! Who of us still retains the innocence of our childhood? Have we not all known
better days, better days of purer feeling, of
greater spirituality, of holier desires, loftier
aims, of a shrinking from evil, succeeded by a
dreary winter-time of coldness and torpor, and
indifference and tampering with sin, and stilling
of conscience, and harbouring of evil in our
minds? When in the impressionable season of
our youth we consecrated with prayer the solemn
vow of Confirmation, what good resolutions we
made for the future! God's Spirit seemed to
pour in upon our souls in a full tide of quick-

ened aspirations, in a rush of emotion, which if only we could have retained it, must, we feel, have armed us, as in a coat of mail, against all the future assaults of Satan! But compare your present spiritual condition with that day in your past life which you can never forget. Do you not often wish that you could feel and think and pray now as you felt and thought and prayed in days gone by?

Or think again of the bed of sickness on which you were for some time laid. God called you aside out of the multitude. It was He who laid you very low. You were brought during that sickness much nearer God than you had ever been before. In health you had forgotten Him; in sickness He called you to remembrance. In the chamber of sickness Temptation was kept at a greater distance. God's Spirit plied you with self-accusing thoughts. Your prayers were fervent where before they had been cold; earnest where before they were only half in earnest. The awakened sense of sinfulness opened your eyes to the need of a Saviour, and to the preciousness of His great salvation. The Word of God was read to you in many a quiet hour, and interpreted to your more understanding mind amidst the solemnities of an uncertain

illness. The season was one of expulsion of
evil; it was one of purifying, sanctifying, re-
forming influence. But what since then? With
restored health and returning buoyancy of spirits, with renewed physical health, have you not
declined from the warmth and sincerity of those
better resolutions? Have not the deposed powers
of evil stolen back and re-asserted their old
dominion? Has there not been a relapse from
that once better state?

Recall the thoughts awakened and suggested
by some bitter sorrow, some saddening bereavement, some heart-breaking cross in your past
life. God's voice, by His Spirit, spoke earnestly
and impressively to you in that hour of sorrow
and trial. It spoke as It had more than once
before spoken to you. You felt at the time that
God *was* speaking to you. For a while also His
voice seemed to inspire you for good. The presence, the fact of Death at your own door, within
your own home, opened your eyes to the reality
of Death and of another world. The desire of
re-union with that which you had so tenderly
loved, encouraged resolutions to lead a more
religious life consistently with the desire of
· re-union in that better world where there is
no more death and no more separation. But

since then has there not been a relapse ? The vividness of these feelings—has it not passed away with the lapse of time ? Earnest for a while, sincere for a while, we have been so only for a while. We return to our former state like the bent bow after the severe strain and tension. Looking back in more mature life on our youth, when we were frequent on our knees, frequent at the Lord's Table, do we not feel that we are not now what we were then ? Have we not known and enjoyed a comparative freedom from sin, through the influence of a con-straining power which we are compelled with sorrow to confess is not as influential with us now ? Who is the man that has so repented of past evil that he does not sometimes cast a han-kering look behind him ? Who has his heart so braced, and has so renounced the world as never to fall beneath its allurements ? Who, as he kneels down before the great Searcher of all hearts, has not daily to confess not only his short-comings, but also his *backslidings ?*

Shall we think lightly of this, brethren, as if it were of little moment ; as if because thus far no perceptible grievous consequences have flowed from our backslidings we may dismiss the sub-ject from our minds ? What is there that the physician so much fears as a relapse after a dangerous illness ? There may be recovery up to a certain point. If proper care and precaution be taken, that recovery may result in restoration to health. But if there be any imprudence, any neglect of proper precautions, if the patient presume upon the symptoms of returning strength and overtax his powers through over-estimating them, a relapse ensues, and a relapse is generally fatal. The sick man, so near recovery, sinks under the renewed attack which he is not equal to resist. To say of one recovering from a dangerous illness that he has had a relapse, is to speak of his approaching end.

It is so with the immortal soul. It is so with our spiritual life. To fall away from grace given is spiritually to die. For the danger of falling away from grace lies not only in the forfeiture of blessing, the withdrawal of grace, the clouding of the conscience, the hiding of God's countenance, but inasmuch as a besetting sin becomes only more and more besetting as it is indulged, so the powers of resistance become proportionably weakened. The sinfulness is aggravated by the fact that it is doing despite to the Spirit of grace. The temptation is re-admitted into the heart once " swept and garnished," but void of all former

and better convictions.   There is less excuse for
it. Providential dispensations have failed of their
appointed end, and have been turned from their
purpose.   God, consistently with His method of
dealing, has no resources left.   His Spirit does
not always strive with, never coerces man.
And into one thus weak and defenceless the
restless spirit, as to some old haunt, returns.
" I will return unto my house whence I came
out.   Then goeth he, and taketh to himself
seven other spirits more wicked than himself,
and they enter in and dwell there, and the last
state of that man is worse than the first."

In connexion with this subject, brethren, and
in view of this season of Lent, it will be well
briefly to consider some few of the more common
causes of such relapse in baptized Christians,
and this consideration will suggest the safeguards
to secure us against them.   The first and most
obvious, perhaps, is *wilful, presumptuous sin*—
sin which is against light and knowledge.   We
can probably all of us recall some wilful inatten-
tion to the warnings of conscience, some decided
act of our own mind to do wrong.   We have
earnestly desired something which we knew it
was not right under the circumstances to have
or enjoy.   We have put ourselves deliberately in

the way of temptation. We have sought out opportunities of sinning, frequenting scenes where we knew beforehand that temptation would meet us. Is it any wonder that we fall? Is it any wonder that the Spirit of God should depart from us, and should leave us alone to commit the self-chosen, deliberately planned, deliberately acted sin? How many men are carrying about with them a bosom sin! To all outward appearance in health, this bosom sin is as a cancer eating into their spiritual life, the secret of their spiritual decay and death. Such are the sensual, the unchaste, the proud, the intemperate. To sin thus wilfully; to steel the heart against all better convictions; to persist in some course of life which God can never sanction or bless; to forget for all practical purposes the warnings of sickness, the solemn voices of bereavements, the self-chidings of sorrow, the better days and happier hours of the past, and to rush headlong once more into a vice or indulgence, to the danger of which these dispensations were intended mercifully to open our eyes—what is this but to court and even to solicit the return of the Evil Spirit in sevenfold strength? And surely the last state must be worse than the first —worse far than the first.

And whence comes it that men sin wilfully? Whence comes it, that although we have once "tasted of the heavenly gift," and the Holy Ghost has been given to us in all its hallowing influences and better inspirations, and to all appearance some lust has been conquered, the strength of some vice crippled, the power of some habit broken, whence comes it that not only does the Holy Spirit forsake us, but that all these sinful desires and feelings are revived within us, and endued with sevenfold strength? It is, we answer, through the force of habit. The cure has not been complete and radical. It has only been partial and superficial. All these better feelings and convictions have lasted no longer than the occasion which excited them. They have deceived us by their very character into the belief that we were at heart what, judging by these feelings, we thought ourselves to be. The evil spirit has not been exorcised and cast out for ever. We have failed to cherish our better convictions and to pray for their abiding permanence. We have not sought to deepen good impressions—transient in themselves—in appointed means of grace. We have not carried with us into our future life the chastening, humbling, saddening reflections of the sick room, of the chamber of death, of the hour of anguish. Thus, by little and little, through relaxed vigilance, want of care and precaution, by returning to the world which we had renounced; by slackening of good intentions; hankering after past evil and shrinking from the severity of the discipline of a self-denying life, we have relapsed. The soul, not possessed by the Spirit, left void, empty and untenanted, is quickly taken possession of by the Evil One, and then it is with us as with some stream which has been dammed up and restrained within certain limits, for which no outlet has been provided, which has not been diverted into other safer channels. The pent-up waters burst through and over the inefficient barrier, the mighty flood carrying all before it impetuously, pours desolation over the fairest scenes of nature. Then it is with us as with the patient, who trusting too much to the mere symptoms of recovery, overtaxes that little strength which is but weakness, and succumbs, when almost grasping life, to that renewed attack which forces him back to his bed of sickness, and hurries him beyond all hope of recovery to his grave.

If this be so, what are our safeguards? It is

true the passages in Scripture are very awful
which speak of the consequences of falling from
grace, of backsliding, of returning to old and
sinful courses. But so long as there is life there
is hope. So long as the faintest pulsation of the
beating heart can be felt, so long as the quivering
pulse yet throbs, so long it is in the power of
God to raise us up from what physicians may pro-
nounce a fatal sickness. It is only when the heart
ceases to beat, and the pulse no longer throbs,
and not a spark of life animates the lifeless
corpse, that we can say that all hope of recovery
is past. So the opportunities of salvation cease
only with life itself. The fountain opened for
sin and for uncleanness is always open on this
side of the grave. The fallen, the sinful, the
penitent may find mercy and grace to help in
time of need. Though no one would encourage
another to trust to a death-bed repentance,
nor to postpone that, which ought to be the
earnest work of his whole life, to the last and
uncertain hours of a mortal sickness, yet the
saving efficacy of Christ's death, as applied by
faith, may reach the soul even in this extremity
to its eternal salvation. It has been well said
that the malefactor on the Cross was forgiven,
once that none might despair, but only once that

none might presume. If you would be preserved
and kept from falling, turn your recollection to
good account. If you have ever consciously
grieved God's Spirit, pray Him to return.
Realize the agency, the work of God's Spirit.
Pray for It day by day, not for to-morrow, which
may never come; but day by day, as you ask
for daily bread, that He will take possession of
your frail, erring, sinful nature; that He will
not forsake you, but that He will go with you
throughout the day into all your occupations and
amidst those scenes and paths in which temptation lies, and in which temptation has more than
once already overcome you. Cherish the motions
of God's Spirit. Try to retain them. Whenever
you are sensible of them, whenever you feel that
He is working in you, and putting into your
heart good desires, thank God for this token of
His nearness. Encourage and foster these good
desires in your own private prayers, by the
study of God's Word, in the Holy Communion
by means of which Satan's power is now hemmed
in and neutralized. Seek with all your heart
and soul Him whose power is greater than
Satan's power. Christ will give you of His
strength by which He vanquished Satan. He is
able to succour them that are tempted. "He can

have compassion on the ignorant and on them
that are out of the way." The remembrance of
past sins and of many falls, the consciousness of
present weakness, as it cannot fail to excite
yearning for deliverance from the cruel bondage
of sin, ought to lead you more to Him " Who
taketh away the sins of the world." As it
humbles us in our own eyes, and shows us how
little good we have in ourselves, so this recollection, this rueful experience, should make us prize
yet more His great salvation. It should make
us more anxious that the benefit of His Death
and Passion should reach our souls. To whom
indeed can we go, when, with the disciples, we
are in danger of turning back and walking no
more with Him, but to Him Who is our merciful
High Priest, Who has the words of Eternal Life,
Who alone can keep us from falling ?

And in so far as your will is concerned
in avoiding the perils of relapse, beware of
remembering past sins without repentance.
Beware also of making excuses for present
faults without striving to correct them. For
this is only to encourage and strengthen the
faults we are attempting to excuse. From this
nothing can come but a gradual declining of
the heart, because the corrective power of reli-

gion is weakened by constant self-excusing.
Beware also of those particular forms of temptation which have already once held you in their
power or sapped your good resolutions. "Have no
fellowship with the unfruitful works of darkness,
but rather reprove them." No one would say
that one who is penitent and watchful could not
be restored. God's mercies in Christ are great.
"He willeth not the death of a sinner, but that
all should repent and be saved." As we pray in
our comprehensive Liturgy that He would raise
up them that fall, so we, who have often sinned
in years past, may take comfort in the thought
that though our life must be always saddened
and made more grave by these remembrances, it
is not therefore unblessed, if we have, through
our falls, been cleansed from evil, incited to
deeper devotion, lowlier repentance, more earnest
prayer, a livelier watchfulness. So far from ever
wishing to forget our past sins, we should feel
that it is rather an act of God's mercy to leave
the burning remembrance of the conflict and
the defeat imprinted upon our conscience, so as
to bring us to present repentance and to final
pardon. And so far from ever murmuring at
any of His dispensations of chiding and sorrow,
we should rather retain in our minds a grateful

sense of the means by which He has mercifully sought, and is seeking to bring us back who were wandering far from the fold of safety, and to turn our erring feet once more into the paths of life.

SERMON VIII.

MATT. xii. 30.

" He that is not with Me is against Me : and he that gathereth not with Me scattereth abroad."

" WITH Me;" " against Me ;" " gathering with Me ;" " scattering abroad." These are weighty words, brethren. They are of deep significance taken in connexion with the fundamental principles and central thought of Christianity, as the remedial system planned for the recovery of a ruined world. For there are two influences and powers actively concerned with the souls of men, in direct antagonism the one to the other, viz. good and evil. On the one hand, there is the whole world lying in wickedness, retaining the

[1] Preached at the Special Services held in Westminster Abbey, March 10, 1861.

scar of the primeval curse, over which the apostate spirit is permitted to exercise a temporary
dominion; and, on the other hand, there is that
kingdom which the Son of God came down
from the highest heavens to establish on earth,
an invisible kingdom of holiness, of which He
Himself laid the foundation stone, in His own
sacred person opposing the power of Satan, and
wresting from him the sceptre of a long un-
disputed sway. Single-handed, not with carnal
weapons, not with the armed legions of a celestial host, but through the resistless might of
the indwelling Spirit of God, He waged un-
sparing war with evil in whatever form it was
presented to His all-discerning mind. This was
His distinct mission. This was His appointed
work. Alike over the material and spiritual
world He asserted the authority and majesty of
a higher will. From the cradle to the grave,
even in the very sepulchre in which He lay
entombed, His pure spirit wrestled with the
enthralling spirit of evil. His whole earthly
life was one sustained, self-sacrificing effort to
reclaim the souls of individual men, and to
found a spiritual kingdom of individual Christians through the sheer force of His own bright
example. Hallowed to memory is the land

which was the scene of His beneficent labours.
Every village, every spot in the Holy Land is
invested with a sanctity which time can never
lessen. His power is no longer visibly exercised amongst men. His voice is no longer
heard exhorting to holiness. We cannot gaze
on that Divine countenance, which has in all
ages challenged the highest conceptions of the
artist. His personal influence, in its more sensible exercise, is withdrawn, yet the influence
of His teaching and example is more largely
felt with each succeeding year. Its reality is
attested by the gradual spread of Christianity.
The restoring principle of the Gospel is confessed wherever it has thus far penetrated, and
whatever region of darkness it has illumined.
That great contest which He initiated has never
ceased. He has bequeathed to all posterity the
solemn charge of carrying on the work which
He inaugurated; of building up the Kingdom
which He has founded. In every country,
blessed with the knowledge of the "truth as
it is in Jesus," every individual is in his degree
responsible for the furtherance of Christ's Kingdom, and has his opportunities of hindering or
advancing the sacred cause. The words of my
text were spoken in refutation of the blasphemy

of those who attributed the miracles Christ
wrought to Satanic agency, and as an argument
against the idea of collusion between Himself
and Satan. This is their primary signification.
There is, however, an interpretation of which
they are susceptible viewed in reference to our
personal, individual share in advancing the
cause of Christianity, "He that is not with Me
is against Me; and he that gathereth not with
Me scattereth."

If these words are of such significance viewed
in connexion with Christianity as a scheme for
the recovery of mankind, as the only means with
which we are acquainted adequate to effect that
object, how momentous are they when we reflect
that by a necessary law of our being we individually advance or hinder the increase of
Christ's kingdom on earth! The mission of
every man,—whether he fulfil that mission or
not,—is, according to his ability, opportunity,
and means, to assist in leavening society, and in
bringing about that grand moral reformation
which is to precede the second coming of our Lord.
Every man, ere he quits this world, has been
during his life and in his generation a source of
strength or of weakness to the cause of Christ.
He has gathered with Christ, or he has scattered

abroad. By his own example, by the general tenour of his conduct, as seen and observed by those with whom he is necessarily brought into frequent contact, he has exercised an influence for good, or tainted the moral atmosphere with the contagious poison of his own vicious example. It cannot be otherwise. There is no one, in whatever sphere he moves, be it the highest or humblest in the social scale, who is altogether without any degree of influence in the world. The law of human influence is deeper, more real than we are prone to suspect or allow. Society is the aggregate of individuals, and individual minds impart to society its tone and character. Consciously and unconsciously we contribute individually to the sum total of national piety or national impiety. That which gives us this influence for good or for evil is, that, as moral beings, we are endowed by the Creator with certain moral qualities, which absolutely require the presence of other men in order that they may be called into exercise. The existence of our fellow-creatures in all the varied circumstances, conditions, and relationships of life draws out of us, develops these essential qualities. God has seen fit to bestow upon us certain faculties which may be employed to the very noblest ends, or perverted and misused, so as not only to degrade our own selves, but—because of the mysterious threads which constitute the network of society—to affect other minds with pernicious effect also. That then which constitutes this individual responsibility is, that we possess qualities of a nature which cannot but act and react upon the outward world of our fellow-men, and that these qualities are susceptible of a healthy or un-healthy exercise. Influence of some kind is ever and actively going forth from us. We are at all times the passive recipients of influence from others. The truth taught by this text, in connexion with this fact, is very important, and it is this—that this influence is either for good or for evil. There is no such thing as being neutral in this matter. Every good man has a power and influence belonging to himself which others feel when he least suspects it. Every bad man has in himself a fund of evil by which he is ever contaminating those around him, even when he has not a thought to do them an injury. Simply to *be* is to exert an influence. The laws and condition of our being render it impossible that we should stand by inactive, disinterested lookers-on, and not take and have an individual, proper part in that great warfare which is being waged between vice and virtue, of which this world is the theatre and stage.

Considering the contracted limits of our own sphere in the world, viewed in contrast with the vast area of the habitable globe, individual influence may seem no more real or possible than the dream of the enthusiast. When the eye ranges over a map of the world, comprising so wide an extent of territory, and then contemplates the circumscribed spot on which we have our temporary residence, or when we think of the countless millions of the human race widely separated by intervening seas, scattered over the surface of this terrestrial planet, and then reflect on the comparative fragment of time during which the longest lived is brought in contact with his fellow-creatures, individual example may appear useless, hopeless, and vain. If again we look abroad and call to mind the multitudes still unenlightened, or the mass nearer home who are living without God in the world, individual efforts may seem impotent, powerless, utopian. But this is to shut our eyes to, and to forget a great fact which obtains alike in the material and moral world. Few facts are more remarkable, and admit of more and varied illustration, than that of the utilization of minute life [2]. God has so ordered it that the greatest and most wonderful results shall flow from the united exertion and co-operation of individual organisms. Look at the vast coral reefs in the Southern seas. How have these attained their magnitude? Humboldt affirms that the coral reefs have attained such a magnitude in the Pacific as even to modify the bed of the ocean, and contribute largely to the formation of new continents, compared with which the boasted monuments of man, such as the great wall of China or the pyramids of Egypt, sink into insignificance [3]. These vast masses of calcareous rock have been secreted in the course of ages by generations of tiny architects, labouring assiduously during their ephemeral life amidst the waters of the deep, each individual zoophyte contributing to the general result. The sea-shore is but the sum total of separate individual grains of sand. In the dense Australian forests each individual leaf deepens the shade. The ocean, laving with its fathomless waters distant shores, is indebted for its vastness to individual drops of water. The

[2] See a recent and very interesting work on this subject, by Dr. Phipson. (Groombridge and Son.)

[3] Humboldt's Views of Nature.

very light, which streaming down from the cloud-
less sky illumines the world, is the aggregate
of separate, individual luminous atoms which
compose the rays. Not more true is this of the
natural than of the moral world. These are but
facts, observable in Nature, illustrative of the
principle on which all great moral results are
also effected. What the polyp is to the coral
reef; the grain of sand to the sea-shore; the leaf
to the forest; the drop to the ocean; the luminous
atom to the sunbeam, such are we individually
to the mass of the human race. And even in
this aspect of the importance and place of the
individual, judging from the analogies of the
natural world, there is a great truth implied in
the words of our Saviour :—

*" He that is not with Me is against Me ; and
he that gathereth not with Me scattereth abroad."*

Is not the truth set forth in this passage confirmed by what we see ourselves every day of the
force and power of example? The man who
fears his God ; who in the crowded as well as
solitary walk of life carries with him the thought
of His All-seeing Eye ; whose religion is not of
an ostentatious character, but the sober piety
which leavens his conversation and controls his
conduct ; such an one recommends the truth to

all with whom he is brought in contact. He
"adorns the doctrine of God our Saviour in all
things." He is "an epistle read of all men."
He may not enjoy large opportunities of propa-
gating the Gospel, but he is in his own way a
missionary of the Cross. He may not bid a long
adieu to home and friends, and in his fervent
zeal for Christ, cross pathless oceans and burning
deserts, risking his precious life amidst all the
perils of a foreign land, but he as effectually and
as truly assists in advancing Christ's kingdom
by his consistent conduct in that smaller sphere
in which he moves. Few can altogether resist
or be indifferent to the constraining influence of
good example. The man of truth, honesty,
high principle, earnest piety, attracts others by
a kind of spiritual magnetism. In all grades
and aspects of society this holds good. A nation
takes its tone from the private life of the Sovereign who rules over it. If a court be dissolute,
the nation becomes licentious. If the fear of
God be known to rule the throne, and piety is
encouraged by those who bear earthly rule, the
people will be a righteous people. The statesman
who legislates for the glory of God and to promote the well-being of his country encourages
the same sacred cause. The man of noble birth

who lends his name, and influence, and presence
to those societies and schemes whose immediate
object is some spiritual good in connexion with
Christianity, not only contributes directly much
real strength to religion, but indirectly, by the
force of his example. The man of trade and
business who, in the prosecution of his lawful
calling, scorns to stoop to dishonourable means
by which to increase his profits, and prefers
straightforward dealing to gains acquired at the
expense of principle, in his own unobtrusive
way is working with God, is gathering with
Christ. To him the shop and mart and ex-
change afford a legitimate sphere in which he
may exercise an influence for good. The young
man, who placed in a situation of trust and
responsibility, avoids the temptations incident to
his position, and at the close of his day of labour
can approach his Maker with " a conscience void
of offence toward God and toward man," is also
contributing in his degree to the furtherance of
Christ's kingdom. We may narrow within still
more contracted limits the sphere of opportunity,
in which we may be instrumental in carrying out
the object Christ had in view. The parent has
an influence over his child, such as no one else can
have, which cannot but deeply affect the child's

future. The plastic soul of the child is continually receiving impressions. We sow in the virgin soil of their susceptible minds the seeds of Christian principle or the tares of a future noxious and strangling growth. The master in the household sets an example, often unconsciously, which the servant notes, and if he be a Christian man his influence will be felt for good in his household. Are there not, do we not all feel that there are countless opportunities of daily occurrence, more or less suited to our individual capacities, by availing ourselves of which our life may be a life of Christian usefulness in the world? Who can truly say that he has never met with them? Who can say he cannot find them or that they are denied him? The work God calls upon us to do may not be that which shall astound the world with the eloquence of a Massillon or Whitfield. It may not be that which shall inaugurate a new era with a Knox or Luther. It may not be such as shall raise the character of a nation with a Wilberforce. It may be no more than the silent, unobtrusive, daily, common-place routine work of *doing your duty* in a family, of exhibiting Christian graces, and cultivating the Christian character in that home which is to us all a lesser world, where unity is so essential to happiness, and where, more than any where else, the love of Christ should dwell and reign supreme. You may win a soul to Christ in an occasional visit to the poor man's humble home, and sitting by the sick bed of the pauper may be the bearer to him of the message of salvation. You may do something for Christ by rebuking profanity when uttered in your hearing; by a bold, courageous profession of Christ at the risk of ridicule; by not being ashamed to be surprised on your knees in prayer; by avoiding scenes where you must lay aside your Christian character if you enter them; by declining the companionship of those whose acquaintance is not desirable, and who would only lead you astray. The husband may influence the wife for good; the wife may be the means of saving her husband; the purer mind of the sister may act with salutary effect on the headstrong passions of youth; the child's example of innocence may affect by its very simplicity the rougher, sterner nature of the father. Not only in various ways, but also in various degrees we may exercise an influence for good in the world. One in this way, another in that way; one on a larger and more extended scale, another in a smaller and more limited, we may each and all be collecting, as the Greek word συνάγων implies, be gathering in with Christ, reaping the golden grain to the harvest of souls.

If all this be true of the attractive influence of good example; if it be a matter of familiar experience that we may shed around us an influence for good, and co-operate with Christ in the work of restoration, the converse of this is equally true. Of the magnetized bar of iron one end attracts, the other end repels. As we may be individually instrumental in winning souls, so we may be individually instrumental in hindering the salvation of our fellow-men. If we are not on the side of God in this world, decidedly, avowedly, we side with Satan. If we do not gather with Christ, we not only are doing no good, but more than this, we *scatter*. The words "*gather*" and "*scatter*" (σύνάγων, σκορπίζει) are borrowed as metaphors from agriculture. The one means "*collecting the grass into heaps,*" the other "*scattering it abroad.*" Scattering! How true this expression is of the influence and the effect of evil example! How contaminating evil example is! It is like some subtle poison infused into the blood which you cannot eliminate. It is like some foul, noxious gas which infects the atmosphere with fatal, contagious effect. It is like the germ of corruption, spreading further and further with putrefying taint. It is like mildew, which blights the fairest promise of fruit. These are only images of the effect of evil example—of influence for ill. I am not speaking now of idolatry and superstition as opposed to Christianity; of heresies as they exist to the prejudice of truth; of infidelity openly avowed or insidiously encouraged; of publications which are made the vehicle of views hostile to religion and morality; of opinions set forth in print as the deliberate, well-considered opinions of those who should, from their position, be pillars of the Church in which they minister, and not its worst enemies. These in a more general way, through the wide diffusion of a cheap literature and that extensive circulation which our highly civilized life so largely facilitates, are all means toward the same end. They tend to "scatter." Doubt is originated and suggested where no shade of doubt was before, or it is confirmed where it had already existed. The mind is unsettled and disturbed. Scepticism, not in the sense of free inquiry, but in the invidious sense of a state of general disbelief, is encouraged. Faith is made

to give place to Reason. Through the pernicious
tendency of erroneous teaching, men question in
matters of faith which are above their reason,
and hesitate to accept that which God conceals
from the wise and prudent and reveals unto
babes. It is not this on which I would now
dwell, though there is much in the present
day of this kind of evil influence, and not a
little cause for anxiety. I am considering rather
that personal influence which proceeds from character — that insensible influence which flows
forth from us unbidden, over and above the
deliberate and outward endeavours of good or
bad men. History furnishes us with striking
illustrations. and instances of the effect which
the vices of one man have had on the age in
which he lived. There will always be those
who will view these vices with disgust and
abhorrence, but there are too many who only
want an example to give a *quasi* sanction to
their own course of life. Many who would
be restrained from sin through the force of
a counteracting influence, or through fear of
public opinion, are encouraged when they see
men in a position superior to their own, men of
rank and title, of high birth and affluent means,
dissolute, irreligious, and profane. We all know

too well how seductive and how alluring sin
is : how very easily we allow ourselves to be
led astray; how often the voice of conscience,
the sense of duty and avowed principle are
made to give way to passion, and desire, and
inclination. If we are not active in the cause
of good, our very inactivity, our supineness, our
indifference often operates so as to deter others
from that activity to which they incline. "We
do not do this and that, why should they ?"
Or, " Such an one has no scruples, why should I
have any ?" " Such an one sees no harm in a
particular line of conduct ; he never attends the
House of God; is never seen at the Table of the
Lord ; rarely, if ever, reads his Bible; is not a
man of prayer, and yet is outwardly prosperous ;
why need I be more particular, more serious
minded, more devout, more prayerful than he ? "

Is not this to scatter ? Is it a light thing,
brethren, to take the name of God in vain ? It
will shock the ears of some, but the oath falls on
the ear of others, and how many of the younger,
hearing the profanity and blasphemy proceed
from the lips of elders, think it must be a manly
thing to swear? Is the unseemly jest a trifling
thing ? It will offend one jealous for the honour
of his God, but it will elsewhere excite a shout

of boisterous mirth, and be quoted as something pointed and clever. Is the unchaste life a light thing? No. There will be those who will instinctively shrink from the companionship of one who leads it, but there are many more with whom it is no secret that one who moves in good society, and has a fair reputation in the world, is all the while sinning against the laws of God, and they follow his example. Study the history of crime. Nothing is less romantic than crime. The forger, the gambler, the drunkard, the thief, the adulterer, the murderer, are all instances of the effect of evil association and of evil influence. He has learned his dishonesty; received his first lessons in fraud; been persuaded to risk his money; led on from small beginnings by others; yielded to solicitations, until the power of resistance was no longer his. He has received an education in vice that terminates in an ignominious death. The confession of criminals on the eve of their execution bears witness to the power of example to ruin and destroy. It is terrible as it is mysterious to think how much it is in our power to benefit or injure others; how much it is in our individual power to save a soul from death, or to ruin it for ever and for ever. You have seen a stone cast into the calm and glassy lake. It was but a small pebble that was thrown. Yet watch the effect. Outwards from where it fell, circle upon circle radiates as from a centre—widening and widening still—embracing at last the whole lake. The philosopher will tell you that the whole of the extent of the lake is sensibly agitated by that apparently trivial cause. Such is our individual influence in the world of men. It may appear insignificant and small, but, like that pebble, it is cast into the ocean of human existence. It affects the circle nearest to us; it widens out beyond the limits of our own home; it continues to extend itself so as to embrace and affect posterity; it will go on widening until at last the wave reaches and breaks on the distant shore of eternity!

Brethren, the reflection which naturally suggests itself on a review of this subject is one which no honest man should dismiss from his mind without serious examination. It is this— Am I with Christ or against Christ? Am I myself gathering with Him, or scattering abroad? Am I known in the world at large and in the circle of my private acquaintance as one whose example may be safely followed, as one of consistent piety, as one who will not only not do or say that which is wrong, but who may be depended upon as always doing that which is right? Is your name one which when mentioned commands deserved respect? Is it so identified with the cause of Christ that it carries with it weight and influence? Does religion meet with encouragement at your hands, not only by the support you give to charitable institutions, and by the active interest you take in every measure of practical good; not only, I say, in this, which is no certain test of piety, but in a less ostentatious, more convincing way: the profane man will not utter the oath in your presence; the vicious will not boast to you of his vices; the dishonest will not meet your eye; the impure will be ashamed to confess his life; the worldly-minded will not court or care for your society? Is your conversation such as becometh the people of God? Is your household a household fearing Him? Do you set your children, your servants, an example for good? Are you anxious for their spiritual welfare? Do you give them sufficient opportunity for attending the House of God on the Sabbath, and availing themselves of the privileges of the Christian covenant? Are you a man of much secret prayer? Are you endeavouring to live

near to God, united by faith with Jesus Christ
as the branch with the vine, blessed in your
inmost soul with the abiding presence of His
Spirit, so that you shed around you consciously
and unconsciously an influence for good?

Or, or is it all the other way? If not openly
and avowedly, yet by a kind of tacit consent and
acquiescence, is evil encouraged by you? Is your
religion all outside, assumed for appearance' sake;
formal, routine religion, void of all spirituality?
Are you to be found habitually in scenes where
you could not meet God? Not cultivating
holiness yourself, nor circumspect in your own
conduct, are you known as one who is not over
nice, or scrupulous, or conscientious? Do you
set an example which it would not be safe to
follow, and which proves a stumbling-block in
another's way to Heaven? Do you scatter
around you that influence for ill which neutralizes
the work of God's grace in the soul, and is
directly antagonistic to the restoring principle
of Christianity?

In this, as in every thing else touching our
practice, our own conscience must decide and
answer for us. This is a question of every-day
life. It is also a strictly personal question.
We cannot plead want of opportunity. Oppor-

tunity lies all around us.   But this opportunity
is also passing away.   Swifter than the weaver's
shuttle speed the fleeting hours, and those fleeting moments which make up our individual life.
The opportunities of Christian usefulness, the
opportunities of advancing Christ's kingdom
cease with life.   It is this fact which makes the
alternative of being "with Christ," or "against
Christ" so momentous.   No one of us here, in
this vast throng of men, may leave this temple in which we are assembled and say that
he is not concerned in this matter.   Were there
no future life to come; were there no resurrection from the dead; no judgment-throne to be
set, before which we must individually appear,
we might speak of our influence for good or evil
as an "idle tale."   But it is the fact, and the
thought, and the prospect of that coming future
which invests this passage of Scripture with
most solemn significance.   At the close of this
earthly life, ere the soul is summoned shortly
hence, in the awful solemnity of that last hour,
what will our reflections be?   Shall they be
something of this melancholy, remorseful nature:
"My day is now fast drawing to its close.   I
am about to appear before God.   I feel that I
have done little or nothing to His glory while

I lived. I have not fulfilled the end and purpose of my individual existence and creation. I now see what opportunities I have let slip. I now see that Christ has not had in me a faithful, earnest, zealous, active fellow-worker; and alas! it is now too late!"

Or shall it be with chastened thankfulness of spirit: "My work is ended, and I am about to enter into my rest. 'I have fought a good fight, I have finished my course, I have kept the faith: henceforth there is laid up for me a crown of righteousness, which the Lord, the righteous Judge, will give me in that day.' I thank God that He has enabled me by the constant help of His Holy Spirit to glorify Him on earth. I know that He will mercifully pardon the imperfections of my poor service, and accept my humble efforts for the merits and sake of Jesus Christ. It is He alone Who has given me the power, and enabled me to magnify His name. To Him with failing breath will I ascribe all the praise. I commend my departing spirit into His hands, as into the hands of a merciful Creator. Poor as my service has been, yet it has been rendered in all the sincerity of my heart; and there is this word of encouragement which, often inspiring me in life, shall also comfort me in death :—

" ' If any of you do err from the truth, and one convert him ;

" ' Let him know, that he which converteth the sinner from the error of his way shall save a soul from death, and shall hide a multitude of sins [4].' "

> " ' *Tis not for man to trifle.   Life is brief,*
> *And Sin is here ;*
> *Our age is but the falling of a leaf,*
> *A dropping tear.*
> *We have no time to sport away the hours.*
> *All must be earnest in a world like ours.*

> " *Not many lives, but only one have we ;*
> *One—only one.*
> *How sacred should that one life ever be,*
> *That narrow span !*
> *Day after day filled up with blessed toil,*
> *Hour after hour still bringing in new spoil.*"

[4] James v. 19, 20.

SERMON IX.

St. James i. 16, 17.

" *Do not err, my beloved brethren.*

" *Every good gift and every perfect gift is from above, and cometh down from the Father of lights, with whom is no variableness, neither shadow of turning.*"

It is in these words that St. James rebuts the charge that God is the author of evil. For it is one thing, brethren, to speak of evil as permitted by God for some mysterious purpose; it is another thing, and not the truth, to say that God is the author of evil. It is true that temptation is a condition of this our probationary state. It is true that it is an appointed means for our individual sanctification, and where endured in the form of trial, and resisted in the shape of allurement to sin, as it chastens, so, without doubt, it does also purify our nature. To this all the holiest of our fallen race, all most eminent for their piety bear witness; and these are they who have been the most tried and the most tempted.

The whole tenor, however, of Scripture confirms what St. James here declares, that inasmuch as our free will is concerned in temptation, as we are free to resist or to court the evil, so we are wrong whenever we would make God chargeable with our frailty and our sins. Hear what Scripture says: " Let no man say when he is tempted, I am tempted of God : for God cannot be tempted with evil, neither tempteth He any man; but every man is tempted, when he is drawn away of his own lust and enticed" (ver. 13, 14). St. James proceeds to oppose this erroneous idea still further by showing that God is the author of *good*.

There is a remarkable difference, or rather distinction, in the Greek words employed in the text, translated " gift." In the clause " every good gift," the Greek word for " gift " is δόσις; in the clause " every perfect gift," the Greek for " gift " is δώρημα. The one is termed moreover *good;* the other is termed *perfect*. From which,

I am of opinion, we may infer that some of God's gifts are good but not perfect, compared with His more perfect gifts. And this distinction is the key to the meaning of this passage in its practical aspect and application. We may regard the "good gifts" as comprehending and being predicated of all *temporal* blessings; we may regard the "perfect gift" as relating to all spiritual blessings.

The expression "*the Father of lights*" contains most probably a twofold allusion; first to God as the Creator of the celestial luminary bodies, more especially of the Sun, which dispenses light and heat and vivifying influences over all nature; and secondly, to God as the Author of all spiritual blessings and influences. Bengel points out a gradation which is observed in the astronomical metaphors which are here employed, viz. *variableness*, and *shadow of turning*. *Variableness* ($\pi\alpha\rho\alpha\lambda\lambda\alpha\gamma\grave{\eta}$) relating to the "good gift;" *shadow of turning* ($\tau\rho\sigma\pi\hat{\eta}s$ $\dot{\alpha}\pi\sigma\sigma\kappa\acute{\iota}\alpha\sigma\mu\alpha$), denoting even still greater perfection—relating to the "*perfect gift:*" that being the more perfect which has not only no variableness, but not even a shadow of turning.

It is not improbable, considering how largely astrology was studied by the ancients, how firmly the heathen world believed in sidereal influences, and that the Jews themselves were not free from the refined superstition which has not yet died out amongst us, that good and evil were respectively betokened by certain appearances in the heavens, by favourable or inauspicious conjunctions of planets,—it is not improbable that the Apostle would strike at the root of this error,. that temptations proceeded from sidereal influence, by admonishing the Christian converts that from God, the Creator of the starry firmament, nothing but good can and does proceed.

Every temporal blessing, then, comes from God. Of all earthly happiness, and of all that ministers to and produces it, He and He only is the Source and Author.

Brethren, we confess this in theory. We are apt to forget this in practice. We receive many of our blessings as a matter of course, blessings from a fatherly hand, which we have received in the weakness of infancy, throughout our manhood and womanhood; strewn along the path of our more mature life, showered down upon us with unchanging constancy in our old age; and we too often forget the Author of all our good gifts. Too often we know their value

only by their loss. Much of evil as there is in
the world, there is still much good. Much as
there is to harass, to sadden, and to depress,
there is also much to inspire us with gladness
and gratitude. We speak of the alloy in gold
when we speak of our earthly blessings, and it
is true that there is this alloy; but we must
not forget that there is also gold in the alloy.
Even in this fallen world, bearing as it does
many an infallible token of ·its ruined and
degraded condition, God does not deny us
hints, and pledges, and foretastes—even with
all their confessed drawbacks and imperfections
—of what He is really towards us; of what
we are capable; of what is in store for us hereafter.

There are many temporal blessings which are
of this nature. They are evidences, continual
witnesses to us, of God's goodness. And what
are some of these? May we not put Health in
the very forefront of God's temporal blessings?
For what enjoyment of life can there be without
health? Who so unequal to enter into all the
more pure and innocent pursuits and enjoyments
of life as he who is chained down, as it were, to
the bed of lingering sickness, or afflicted with
some chronic complaint, or suffering from pain

which unnerves the whole man, and makes life
itself, even under the most favourable circumstances, almost intolerable ? It is a trite and
yet a true saying that we know the blessing of
health only by its loss.

Are not our different talents, mental endowments, gifts and aptitudes to be reckoned amongst
our temporal blessings? They are sources of
pleasure to ourselves, almost infinite, as we exercise them aright in the acquisition of knowledge,
in the pursuit of that favourite study or particular accomplishment to which we naturally
incline,—aiding us in attaining that success in
life, that position, prosperity, or reputation
·which is only their fair and legitimate reward.
They are sources also of pleasure to others
where we use them with a view to promote the
well-being of our fellow-creatures in the earnest
devotion of those gifts to their good, or where
they serve to lighten some of the darker hours
of life and to shed even the transient gleam of
happiness over the spirit of some less favoured
than ourselves.

Is not the blessing of a clear intellect, of possessing every faculty of the mind in healthy
exercise, of unclouded reason, felt to be great
when we see one afflicted with drivelling

idiotcy, and of defective organization; or when
we pass through the wards of an asylum which
humanity provides for the lunatic of disordered
mind and the raving maniac ?

Shall we not also say that Wealth is a
blessing; that it is one of God's good gifts ? It
is only the covetous and envious man, that looks
with greedy and churlish eye on that which he
does not himself possess, who will deny that,
considering the good which the man of wealth
may do in the world, riches are to be counted
amongst God's good gifts. It is true that
wealth may prove a snare. But has not poverty
its own temptations also ? May not the heart
of the poor man be estranged from God through
murmuring, and envy, and discontent, as effectually and as really as that of the rich man who
makes his wealth his idol and his god ? The
man of ample fortune, who regards his wealth
as a sacred trust, and employs it as a faithful
steward, devoting a due portion to those objects
of charity which need the support of the
wealthier classes; who is considerate towards
his dependents; mindful of his poorer relations;
sympathizes with the necessities of the indigent;
liberal and not close; wisely dispensing his
bounty : surely we may say of him, considering

the happiness he may shed around him, that he is a man blessed of God.

And all other good gifts are from the same loving hand. Friends in life; sympathizing, gentle souls, lightening one another's burdens; brothers and sisters, united to each other by strong, endearing affection; children, to gladden our homes and to soothe declining years; the pleasurable society of mutual friends; the exhilarating interchange of thought with intellectual minds; the consciousness of duties well performed; the inward satisfaction of a rightly ordered, well-balanced mind: all these and many more are sources of earthly happiness. Then to these we may add our daily recurring mercies—our table spread with daily bread; our life preserved from accident and harm; our bodies clothed with raiment; our wearied frames refreshed with "tired Nature's sweet restorer, balmy sleep." And over and above all these temporal blessings we have the sun to rule the day; the moon and the stars to govern the night; we have refreshing rains, moistening dews, genial breezes, the grateful alternative of sunshine and shower; Nature in her revolving seasons, ushering in with each a necessary change; the earth bringing forth her spontaneous fruit in due season ; a most wise and well-considered adaptation of external nature to the constitution and physical organization of man ; and beside all this regular supply of our actual necessities, there are scenes of exquisite beauty to delight the eye; sounds of thrilling harmony to regale the ear; our love of variety is gratified in the lights and shades of landscape ; in the softer beauties or more rugged features of scenery ; in the varied form and delicate painting of bejewelled flowers. All these are God's good gifts. All these come from Him. Nature is but another name for God. All buoyancy of health, all vigour of life is of God. All success, prosperity, and reputation is of God. All comforts and freedom from cankering care and innocent happiness is of God.

Yet these things, good as they are, are not perfect. There are better and more perfect gifts even than these. These are not perfect, because they are temporal and transient. Nothing temporal and transient is perfect. Health, however good, is always liable to injury ; gifts of mind to impairment. Wealth has its temptations and its snares. The friendships of youth may be abruptly severed ; the affection of.

years saddened by the great separation ; adversity
may overtake the most prosperous; the happiest
day comes to a close ; clouds darken the brightest
sky, and, as has been truly said—

" There is even a happiness
That makes the heart afraid."

These earthly sources of happiness then have
their drawback. They are not the best, the
choicest gifts. They are not perfect, even
though they come from the hand of God.

God's perfect gifts are His spiritual blessings;
those which concern not our mortal bodies, but
our immortal souls; those which are eternal in
their nature, and not temporal; those which affect
our everlasting welfare, and not merely transient
good. And what are these spiritual blessings?
First of all, there is to us Christians and to the
whole race of mankind the gift of His dear Son,
Who died that He might redeem a guilty world,
and be a Saviour in the Day of Judgment of
every sinner who believes in His Atonement,
and seeks by faith to have the benefit of
Christ's Passion applied to his own soul. This
is God's best, very best, gift. There is also
the gift of His Holy Spirit to those who ear-

nestly desire and ask for It, to illumine our
minds; to sanctify our hearts; to purify our
sinful nature; to work in us Christian graces
of disposition. There is the gift of His Holy
Word to be the light to our feet, and the lamp
to our paths—"the engrafted Word which is
able to save our souls." There is the gift of
regeneration in the waters of Baptism, developed by after gifts of the Spirit into that
renewal of our nature by which we become
"dead unto sin and new creatures in Christ
Jesus." Shall we not add the blessing of a ·
changed, converted heart; of an awakened,
serious mind; of a tender, sensitive conscience?
There is the privilege of access to God through
Christ in prayer; the blessing of answered
prayer; the blessing *of delay* in answered
prayer. There is the gift of spiritual strength
by which we are enabled to resist temptation; of faith by which we overcome the
world; of all those various graces which adorn
the soul and are the varied developments of
God's Spirit, such as patience in one who
needs patience; humility in another; submission, gentleness, love, temperance in more.
There are appointed means of grace, such as the
Holy Communion, to refresh and strengthen

our souls; the House of God with its privileges;
the preached Word; the sacred day of rest—

" Sweet repose from worldly care,
Day above all days the best,
When our souls for Heaven prepare."

These are God's spiritual and more perfect gifts.
These have no alloy. These are of the holiness
and the perfection of God Himself. Through
these means of grace as we use them, we are
made like unto Him, " changed into the same
image from glory to glory, even as by the
Spirit of the Lord."

One or more thoughts of a practical nature are
suggested by this subject and text. These I
would press on your thoughtful attention. One
is this—that we use these gifts aright; that we
do not abuse them. For that is true which our
great dramatic poet has written—

" Naught so good, but, strained from that fair use,
Revolts from true birth, stumbling on abuse."

There is no one of these gifts which I have
enumerated which may not be abused. The
health which makes us equal to any effort, and
indifferent to a thousand petty cares that harass
the invalid, may be injured by wilful want of

precaution; by pampering the appetites; by softness and luxurious habits of life; by inactive and prolonged repose; by sensual indulgence; by excess, intemperance, and dissipation. To preserve our health, as far as we may, is a sacred duty. Men become prematurely old through excessive mental labour; they shorten their life by that over-fatigue of the brain which induces paralysis, and in a moment of temporary insanity, brought on by over-study, they not unfrequently commit the dreadful criminal act of self-destruction.

So also talents may be perverted and abused. Keen, intellectual vigour, together with an unsanctified heart, is not even a questionable boon. How often the most brilliant genius, the finest powers of mind, the highest intellectual gifts have been exercised in perverting truth, in encouraging infidelity, in hostile and unfriendly assaults on religion! Surely this is only to abuse a good gift. The wit who aims his shafts at all that is best and holiest; the man of intellectual strength who holds up all faith to contempt, who turns piety into ridicule, and makes the Bible the butt of his satire; the trained mind, versed in logic, accustomed to weave and unweave the subtleties of argument, and require demonstrative proof of all assertions; which is impatient of the limits imposed on our finite powers, and accepts nothing which cannot be submitted to the test of reason: do not such as these pervert and misuse those talents, which, if turned to good account, would strengthen the weak, confirm the wavering, guide aright the minds of the more thoughtful and therefore more sceptical, in an age of intellectual vigour such as this?

So again to spend our wealth only on ourselves; to consider our riches as only the means of surrounding ourselves with luxuries, whilst thousands around us want even the *necessaries* of life; to hoard up gains that we may have the reputation of being worth so much in life, and dying worth so much when we quit life; to grudge the trifle to some charity and to be ungrudging in every inclination of our own, what is this but to abuse wealth? What is this but to pervert God's good gifts?

If all this be true of temporal blessings, oh! how much more true it is of spiritual blessings! To live amidst the light and privileges of the Gospel covenant and not to believe in Christ; to be baptized in His Name, and yet to have no desire to be truly His; to hear

continually of His Death on the Cross, and yet
not to accept Him as our Saviour; to know
that "there is none other name given amongst
men, whereby we must be saved," and yet not
daily to pray that we may know Him whom
truly to know is life everlasting, is not this to
abuse God's "perfect gifts?"

To grieve the Holy Spirit by wilful and
habitual sin; to disregard Its admonitions and
resist Its motions; to stifle within us the
voice of Conscience, which is the Voice of God;
never to ask in earnestness for the abiding influences of the Holy Ghost, is not this to despise
the riches of God's goodness?

To read the current literature of the day as
it teems in its manifold forms; to be familiar
with all works of profane literature both of
past and modern times; to be versed in languages; well informed in all branches of secular
knowledge, and yet to neglect to read the Bible;
rarely, if ever, to open its sacred pages in private; to be practically ignorant of that knowledge which maketh wise unto salvation; not
to allow ourselves to be guided by its laws and
precepts in our intercourse with the world, in
doubtful cases, in all nice questions of conscience;
and not to set the very highest value on it,

as the inspired record of the will of God, is not this to abuse it?

And what is habitual neglect of the Holy Communion; neglect of or remissness in private prayer, and of all appointed means of grace, such as the House of Prayer, the blessing of one day in the week for religious and devotional purposes; what is neglect of these but to neglect our soul's health, and to cast aside and be indifferent to all those divine helps which are mercifully vouchsafed us in our momentous conflict with sin? What is this but to imperil our soul's eternal safety? So then the practical thought which lies on the surface of this text, one which you who hear and I who speak may carry away with us into our daily life, is this, that we use aright these temporal and spiritual blessings, the good and perfect gifts which come from above.

We are here also reminded of what we should ask for when we pray, what we should most desire whenever we kneel down in secret before Him Who can supply all our need. Brethren, we often, when we pray, do not know for what we pray. We ask not only amiss, but blindly, and out of the turbulent emotions of the heart. If God were to answer all our prayers, were He to fulfil all our wishes expressed on our knees, how often should we find that we had asked for ourselves, not a blessing, but a curse! The wisdom and goodness of God is shown as much in what He sees fit to deny as in what He vouchsafes to give. Many of you, doubtless, looking back on your past lives, and recalling past wishes, are ready to confess the wisdom of God in withholding what you, in your short-sightedness, once so fervently desired. You feel now and often that it was well God did not grant your prayer. At the time you doubted that God *heard* prayer, because the expected answer did not come. Now you reproach yourself for having ever admitted such a doubt. You feel sure He heard that prayer, which in His infinite wisdom He refused. So, too, when we pray, we too often commence our prayers with the expression of some supposed *temporal* want. We kneel down in anxiety; with a great care absorbing the mind; under the pressure of some necessity, which drives us, as it were, into His presence. Rather, we should begin our prayers with the supplication for *spiritual* blessings. It is wonderful how insignificant our temporal wants will seem compared with our spiritual necessities. It is wonderful, also, how it will calm and soothe the mind thus burdened, to pray for God's strengthening, supporting grace under the momentary trial. "Covet earnestly," says the Apostle, "the best gifts." Temporal blessings God will give you as He sees fit and best for you. Leave all that to His unfailing goodness Who feeds the ravens and clothes the lilies. Your undying soul is of far more worth to you than your perishing body. If He can save the one from eternal death and bless it with eternal glory, surely He can and will provide for the other. The tendency of the age is confessedly to increase all the luxuries of our outward life. With increasing civilization imaginary wants are created, and our whole life becomes more artificial. Every impulse and encouragement is given to the invention and application of some new luxury, some fresh stimulant to the jaded senses.

There are better things, brethren, more en-during, more satisfying than these, which you and I need in view of approaching eternity. Alas! that we should ever forget or lose sight of this! Pray God, if He give you health, to give you also the ready desire to offer yourself, body, soul, and spirit, a reasonable sacrifice to His glory. Pray Him, if He give you talents, to grant you the grace to turn and use them to the furtherance of Christ's Kingdom. Pray Him, if he give you wealth, to give you also a deep sense of its responsibilities and obligations. Pray Him, if He deny you riches, to give you contentment with your lot. Pray Him so to attemper every earthly blessing with some better spiritual grace, that it may never become a snare to you, may never become an idol; that it may never divert your mind from, or lessen your desire for those true and lasting joys which are at God's right hand for evermore.

And lastly, remember this: that with God is no variableness, neither shadow of turning. We live in the midst of incessant change, changes in Nature around us of land and sea. The world in which we live, the very spot on which we stand has, in the long course of ages, witnessed remarkable physical changes. Whole races have become extinct. The very features of the soil are altered. There is change of thought and opinion; change of government; change of politics. In our own system we experience this incessant change. No two days are alike. You cannot to-day reproduce, under exactly the same circumstances, the happiness or sorrow, the joy or sadness of yesterday. Nature in her varied operations and revolving seasons is one scene of change. We have alternate day and night, heat and cold, summer and winter. In the midst of all this God remains unchanged. From Eternity He is the great I Am. From Eternity He has been one and the same God. He would have us stay our minds, amidst all the world's changes, on that unalterable, pregnant truth. As you mark the sun, rising with morning splendour on an awakening world, or setting in his bed of glory in the western heavens; as you watch the various phases of the sister planet, moving in queenly majesty in the starlit firmament, God would have us contrast His unchangeableness with this incessant change. He would have us remember that He is always the same, in His promises, in His threatenings, in His word, in His unfailing goodness. This is to inspire us with confidence in our prayers. This is that practical thought which the Collect for to-day embodies, and which should be the desire of our own hearts, that "among the sundry and manifold changes of the world, our hearts may surely there be fixed where true joys are to be found." .

SERMON X.

Sᴛ. Mᴀᴛᴛʜᴇᴡ v. 6.

*" Blessed are they which do hunger and thirst
after righteousness : for they shall be filled."*

Hᴜɴɢᴇʀ and Thirst. The two strongest, most
powerful Instincts, which belong to, and are
inseparably connected with our present physical
constitution. "Two mighty impulses, beneficent and terrible, sources in the system of
exquisite pleasure and of exquisite pain, motives
to strenuous endeavours, servants to our highest
aims [1];" it is thus that in a recent work on
physiology, these two instincts are described.

In some degree, to some extent, we are all of
us familiar with these sensations. No one of

---

[1] Lewes, "Physiology of Common Life."

us, perhaps, save under very exceptional circumstances, has any idea of that Hunger which borders on and precedes starvation, or of Thirst, when it is nothing less than the most exquisite torture. Our experience of these sensations is in their more agreeable form as the gentle stimulus of appetite; but between this and that Hunger, which, prolonged beyond endurance, becomes a devouring flame; subjugating the humanity in man; impelling men to devour one another greedily; fatal to life; between the mere desire and that intense Thirst which we are told effectually tames the most fierce and refractory of the brute creation, of which the histories of shipwrecks paint such fearful pictures, the agonies of which were felt in their most appalling form in the celebrated imprisonment in the Black Hole at Calcutta; of Thirst, such as this, we are happily ignorant, and between it and desire there are infinite gradations.

We shall, however, enter more fully into the meaning and force of this passage of the Sermon on the Mount, which we have heard read this morning, if we bear in mind the important part Hunger and Thirst play in the animal economy, and if we consider how necessary these two

instincts are, not only to our own personal well-
being, but even to the world at large. For it is
not too much to say that Hunger is the very
fire of life, underlying all impulses to labour,
exciting the human race to all nobler activities
by its most imperious demands. Look where
we may, it is the motive power which sets the
vast array of human machinery in action.
Waste and repair are the alternating, fluctuating
conditions of the human organism. Life is sustained or exhausted in proportion as one or other
of these conditions predominates. Physiologists
assert from accurate observation that we are
momentarily yielding up particles of our bodies
to destruction ; that we cannot wink the eye, nor
raise the hand, without the loss of some particle
of matter ; that every thought, which with lightning speed traverses the convolutions of the brain,
is at the cost of its tissue. It is calculated that
the human body loses daily by waste one twenty-
fourth of its own weight. This daily flux and
waste must be supplied with equal regularity
and constancy, else we should quickly die. The
Creator has endowed us with these two Instincts
which prompt and impel us to satisfy the
cravings of our nature. The felt want must be
supplied, and He furnishes us with Instincts

Q

which incite us to the necessary effort to supply
the want. Food, then, is to our bodies what
fuel is to the furnace. Humbling as the thought
and fact may be, yet so it is, that it is this necessity of food which impels men to all that labour,
physical or mental, which is at all times irk-
some.   It is Hunger that forces us to replenish
the empty furnace and set in motion the fervid
wheels of life.   It is almost a self-evident truth
that were food abundant, easily procured, always
near at hand, civilization would be, if not impossible, yet greatly hindered and retarded.   In
the islands of the Asiatic Archipelago, where
the sago grows wild, where the plantation yields
upwards of one hundred times as much food as
wheat in the same area; where the islander
needs but to hew down the tree which at once
supplies his daily meal, little or no advance is
made from year to year in moral or intellectual qualities, in any of the refinements of
existence. We know that all wheat-producing
countries are the most advanced in civilization,
because more labour is required in the produc-
tion of wheat. The Hindoo, subsisting chiefly
on rice, will not bear favourable comparison
with the European in moral or intellectual
qualities—the staple of his daily diet, rice,

yields one hundredfold, where wheat yields only sixtyfold. Our higher efforts are indissolubly dependent on our lower impulses. As it has been truly said, " Hunger brings the stalwart navvies in orderly gangs to cut paths through mountains, to throw bridges across rivers, to intersect the land with the great iron ways which bring city into daily communication with city. It is Hunger that sits at the loom, which with stealthy power is weaving the wondrous fabrics of cotton and silk. Hunger labours at the furnace and the plough, coercing the native indolence of man into strenuous and incessant activity. And although this seems obvious only when applied to the labouring classes, it is equally, though less directly true, when applied to all other classes, for the money we all labour to gain is nothing but food, and the surplus of food, which will buy other men's labours." The language, then, of our Lord is very remarkable. The terms, the expressions, the metaphors He employs are happy and significant, viewed with reference to these natural instincts, which daily and hourly inspire and impel us to action and labour. We know by experience what Hunger and Thirst incite us to do. It is through the felt force of these

Q 2

sensations, which remind us of the wants created by the wear and tear of our physical life, that we satisfy our physical necessities. As regards that higher, spiritual life which is sustained by angels' food; as regards that life of the soul which can never die, of this He says, " Blessed are they who as ardently pursue and naturally seek after that which is the soul's life, as they seek to satisfy the physical sensations of Hunger and Thirst. Blessed are they which do hunger and thirst after righteousness, for they shall be filled."

Brethren, there is a desire in the human heart corresponding in some sense to this craving of our natural appetites, a desire which we all feel, but which it is difficult to describe. It has been defined as the " craving of infinitude." Our souls are never at rest. We are never satisfied. In all ages the more advanced and thoughtful of the human race have endeavoured to construct an ideal happiness out of even the ruins and broken fragments of this fallen world. They have imagined to themselves, in accordance with their individual tastes and views, and have described in theory the *summum bonum*, the chief good, the highest form of happiness which could satisfy and respond to the instinctive yearnings of the spiritual nature of man. But what philosopher of ancient or modern times has succeeded yet in practically satisfying this craving of our nature, which is restless under any limits, and which finds rest only in the thought of something boundless, infinite, unattainable ? " Is there not," says a thoughtful writer, " a sense of freedom and relief in all that suggests the idea of boundlessness—the deep sky, the dark night, the endless circle, the illimitable ocean ? Hence, too, our dissatisfaction with all that is or can be done. There never was the beauty yet than which we could not conceive something more beautiful. None so good as to be faultless in our eyes. No deed done by us, but we feel we have it in us to do a better. Infinite goodness, a beauty beyond what eye hath seen or heart imagined ; a justice which shall have no flaw, and a righteousness which shall have no blemish; to crave for that is to be ' athirst for God '.'"

There is a boundless, infinite void in the soul of man, and just as " Nature abhors a vacuum," so we seek to satisfy this void ; a strong proof of our immortality, than which there is perhaps

---

[2] Robertson's Sermon on Religious Depression.

none more strong. The soul has infinite capacities. We feel more and more that no limit can be placed to our intellectual capacities. It is only through the imperfection of our present organization that we do not know all that can be known, and as we shall know hereafter. Wide as is the difference spiritually between one of us and an angel of light; vast as is the distance between one in whom the Spirit of God is yet in the germ, and the sainted spirit of a just man made perfect in glory, yet we have the capacity of becoming like God, of being conformed to the mind of Christ; of being "perfect even as our Father which is in Heaven is perfect."

It is after this *perfection* that the soul in its truest moments aspires. Our spiritual instincts, as they remind us of our spiritual wants, so if encouraged and acted upon, will prompt and impel us to seek that satisfying of the craving of our spiritual being of which the Psalmist speaks—

> " *As pants the hart for cooling streams,*
> *When heated in the chase,*
> *So longs my soul, O God, for Thee,*
> *And Thy refreshing grace.*"

In various ways, and with much earnestness of purpose, men seek to satisfy this craving of our nature. All men, even the very poorest and humblest, desire and seek happiness in some form or other. There is an aching void to be filled. There is a something wanting which we have not, and each individual in the vast mass of mankind is busy and intent on satisfying, so far as he may, that felt want—one in this way, another in that way. Hence you have the keen pursuit of Pleasure for the sake of the transient happiness it affords. The day is one round of excitement. It is so arranged, divided, planned, that the hours shall not hang heavily and wearily on the unoccupied hands. As you have seen the butterfly flit from flower to flower, "from morn to dewy eve," and sip from each its drop of honey, so in the gayer world of fashion its votaries flit from one scene of excitement to another, and seek their happiness in this excitement.

Another finds a kind of happiness in the enjoyments and indulgence of sense ; in ease ; in softness ; in luxury ; in all that is understood as sensual gratification ; in those various means and opportunities of gratifying the senses and indulging the animal appetites which wealth can readily procure and which increase with increasing civilization.

There are purer, more innocent, and apparently more rational and satisfactory forms in which this craving is sought to be appeased; in the pursuit, for instance, of Science, Art, and Knowledge; in that studious labour that consumes the midnight oil in storing the mind with information, and communing with the more gifted and intellectual of our race in their posthumous writings; in the effort to obtain worldly fame, reputation, and coveted distinction; in travel; in a favourite employment; in quiet and still home-life with its recreations and endearments. But yet no one of these things really constitutes happiness. These do not, at the best, and even when most fully and innocently enjoyed, come up to the idea of happiness such as may be conceived. The excitement of the theatre, the opera, the ball-room, and nameless diversions of the same exciting nature, is very quickly over. So far from satisfying, these only whet and stimulate the appetite for yet more of the same. At best is not the enjoyment of the ordinary sources of worldly pleasure, of social intercourse and amusement, where happiness has been sought, no more than transient and fleeting? Surely all experience, certainly that of the elder amongst you, and even that of the younger of my hearers, who would naturally be the last to confess it, declares that it is very shortlived.

So, again, with the mere gratification of sense, the indulgence of the appetite in its more gross, or pleasure in its more refined forms of sight and sound, of thrilling harmonies and artistic beauties, this is but momentary also. Nothing is left of it save the remembrance, and this not always the happiest; the pleasure, the charm is evanescent; the gratification passes while we are feeling it.

How much more true is this of knowledge! The longest-lived, how little he learns of all that may be learned! You remember the remarkable saying of one of the highest genius. Newton thus speaks of himself shortly before his death : —"I do not know what I may appear to the world, but to myself I seem to have been only like a boy playing on the sea-shore, and divert- ing myself in now and then finding a smoother pebble or a prettier shell than ordinary, whilst the great ocean of truth lay all undiscovered before me."

So with travel. What scenes of Nature must

still remain unexplored by even the most inde-
fatigable! How small a portion of the globe
may be traversed in the lifetime of an individual! So with those more quiet, less exciting
scenes in which many are content to find their
happiness. The family circle is ere long broken
up. Its various members, entering into new
relationships, pursuing different callings in life,
leave the fireside of their childhood's years. They
cannot ever meet together again under the same
circumstances in this scene of perpetual change.
I do not say that we may not innocently enjoy
much that contributes to our earthly happiness,
even though it be of this fleeting nature. I do
not say that because the purest pleasures of life
are shortlived, we should not therefore enter
into all the happiness they can bring, and thank
God for them. God would have us use these
things, and use them aright. They are misused
when the mind is satisfied to rest in them as
far as it can do so; when it seeks nothing
beyond, nothing better, nothing more enduring.
For the truth is, brethren, that God never intended that we should find our happiness in
these things alone. It is from their very nature
impossible that we should. As we grow older
we learn by experience to find that our real

happiness depends in a very small degree upon
what is external to us. It has its fount in
deeper and hidden sources, like a spring which
through winter cold and summer heat is fringed
with evergreen moss. It is not circumstances
which necessarily make us happy or unhappy.
A well-ordered mind can be very independent
of external circumstances. The man of wealth
and abounding comfort may yet often envy the
poor man's contentment with his frugal board and
peaceful cottage. It is almost a trite and worn
out truth to remind you that the ordinary idea
of happiness is fallacious and unreal. Worldly
pursuits and pleasures, whatever they may do, do
not satisfy us. They are at best only temporary expedients. There is in them nothing
enduring, nothing that responds to the instinctive yearnings of our higher, better, purer
nature. Is it not sublime mockery to call that
happiness which is succeeded by weariness of the
flesh, indolence, frivolous thoughts; not to speak
of heartburnings, envyings, petty jealousies, and
all the worldliness of mind inseparable from
fashionable life? Shall we find it in fortune
and fame? The man of fortune cannot take
with him when he dies one penny of his wealth,
nor the man of fame one leaf of his laurels.

When life's play is over, and the curtain drops, and the lights are extinguished, and the stage deserted, all its actors return to one common level. Earthly distinctions cease with this present economy and system. Happiness, therefore, cannot consist in sublunary distinctions, in merely earthly and temporal advantages. The craving of our nature is not given us without there being also something which corresponds to it; no more than any natural desire exists without its corresponding, appropriate object. There is no rest for our souls apart from God in Christ. Never were truer words uttered than the words of St. Augustine : "Thou madest us for Thyself, and our souls are restless, till they find rest in Thee." It is in this alone that we shall find the satisfying of our deepest wants. Not of any other form of happiness is this promised, but only of that more pure and spiritual, which, as it affects the soul, is eternal and enduring.

"Blessed are they that hunger and thirst after righteousness, for they shall be filled."

What is this righteousness—this δικαιοσύνη —of which our Lord here and elsewhere speaks —" Seek ye first the kingdom of God and His righteousness, and all these things shall be

added unto you?" By this "righteousness" is
denoted "the knowledge and practice of all the
duties we owe to God and man." It is not conformity to a creed, but it is a *state* after which
to aspire. It is the yearning of the soul to be
pure and holy, and Christ-like: "to be found in
Him, not having our own righteousness, but that
which is through the faith of Christ, the righteousness which is of God by faith." It is to
know Christ; to feel the power of His Resurrection working in us with renewing effect; it
is to die daily unto sin, and become new creatures
in Christ; it is to grow daily in grace; to be
clothed in the righteousness of Christ; sanctified
by His Spirit; justified by faith, and made more
and more meet for His everlasting Kingdom.
It is that desire of sanctification and renewal
which every one who reflects on his own vileness
and sinfulness must feel. It is that earnest
longing for pardon of sin, and deliverance from
its cruel tyranny, and inward strength to resist
it, which we can hope for and obtain only
through the merits and for the sake of our Lord
Jesus Christ. It is, in a word, the present
attainment of that, which when this earthly
scene shall have ended,—in that day when the
heavens shall pass away, and a new state of

things be ushered in—shall alone make us meet to share the bliss of God's elect in glory.

This "righteousness" does not consist in many prayers; in hearing many sermons; in the study of the Bible, nor yet in frequent partaking of the Holy Communion. Valuable as these means of grace are to all who use them aright, they are not the end. They are only means towards the end. These feed the flame when once it is kindled, but they are not in themselves the flame. Nor does this "righteousness" consist merely in good actions, which is the opposite extreme to a religion of ritualism and ordinance. It is something more than simply "going about doing good." Good works are the natural fruit of right faith; but the fruit of the tree is something distinct from the life of the tree. Our practical duties are an important part, but only a part, of our religious system. In the presence of so many conflicting opinions, in the vain endeavour, amidst contending schools and harsh controversies, to arrive at truth, there is the tendency to take refuge in mere religious activity, in so-called practical religion, to the exclusion of any definite dogmatic teaching.

This may be a convenient means by which

to save ourselves the trouble of inquiry and the uneasiness of doubt, but one cannot well imagine any practice less satisfactory than that which proceeds on no fixed, recognized principles, and which has no other rule or guide than mere benevolence and natural impulse. Apart from this, however, Scripture, which must be our guide in this important matter, invariably represents this righteousness as consisting in a series of affections and dispositions. " The Kingdom of God is righteousness, and peace, and joy in the Holy Ghost." In the Sermon on the Mount we have in the list of Beatitudes a detailed description of this righteousness, which shows us that it consists in a series of Christian graces wrought in our hearts by the power of the Holy Ghost. It is that internal, hidden life, nourished and sustained by our own prayers, by the concurrence of our own will and heart's desire, by the power of Christ's risen humanity co-operating with us, and developed, not, as we might suppose, in solitude and retirement, not in the still cloister life and in a forced separation from the ordinary pursuits, avocations, and natural ties of our fellow-men, but rather and best in the midst of the busy world, cultivated amidst the jars and collisions, perfected by the trials and antagonisms of our daily life. This too is a state only the more intensely desired, as the ever-changing, ever-shifting scene in which we live, the vanity of all earthly pleasures, which, tried one by one, have proved unsatisfying, the swiftness and shortness of time, and the soul's eternal interests become more and more matter of ripening experience and impressive conviction.

What can you say of yourself in this matter? Do you hunger and thirst after righteousness? Have you ever known and felt this craving of our fallen nature in its purer, better moods? Have you more than merely wished and desired to be like Christ; making no earnest effort to become so? From week to week, from day to day, amidst the throng of thoughts and desires which pass through the mind, is the thought of your soul's necessities, your soul's safety, uppermost, uppermost? Is pleasure, fame, distinction, wealth, praise, position, success in life what you desire, and what you are intently seeking, and only now and then your thoughts are more serious; only now and then occupied with the unseen, eternal world; only now and then turned inwards upon yourself and upward to God? Are you content with a low standard of religion, such as passes current

in the world and with worldly people as
piety, fearing lest you should be thought sin-
gular, over righteous, over scrupulous; fearing
lest your convictions might, if followed, lead you
further than you can yet make up your mind
to go? Do you exercise habitual self-denial,
by which earthly desires are moderated, sinful
feelings mortified, the flesh subdued to the
spirit? And your prayers? Are these for temporal blessings only? When you kneel down in
secret to pray, what is the general tone and
tenor of your prayers? Is it for temporal blessings only or chiefly? For health, preservation,
prosperity, success, some coveted worldly advantage; or do you pray for deliverance from the
yoke of sin? Do you ask for God's Holy
Spirit; for greater purity of mind and heart;
for an increase of faith; for a more real and
sensible union with Christ; for spiritual gifts
and graces, such as we all variously need, if we
would shine as lights in our several homes and
households? A stranger and pilgrim on earth,
are you seeking a city yet to come; living daily
in view of eternity and of the end of life; sanctifying your daily appointed work with daily
prayer; "glorifying God in your body, and in

R

your spirit which are God's?" Is your spiritual
life something more than integrity, uprightness,
generosity, benevolence? Is it a life of spiritual
hopes, and fears, and joys, and aspirations? Are
you choosing now in this your day of grace and
opportunity, as your soul's portion, Him in
Whom there is pardon for the guilty, holiness
for the sinful, rest for the weary, peace for the
disquieted?

Are you—let me ask you further—are you *in
earnest;* not in some vague, indolent, unex-
acting sense, merely *wishing* for happiness,
hoping and trusting that it will at the last be
yours, you scarcely ask how; but desiring it as
you desire food, seeking to satisfy that desire as
a starving man craves the morsel of bread, as
one perishing of burning thirst gasps for the
drop of water to cool his parched lips and
clammy tongue?

Oh! what, think you, must be the death-bed,
and the death-bed reflections of one who only
then thinks seriously of his soul's safety and welfare and necessities, when life is fast ebbing and
he needs all the comfort and assurance of pardon,
to soothe the mind in the immediate prospect of
dissolution? What must be the future of one

—God forbid there be such here—who throughout his or her life, has tried by turns to satisfy
this craving in every way but that which can
alone satisfy it; who has neglected "the one
thing needful?"

The promises. of Scripture are "exceeding
great and precious" to those amongst you who
thus hunger and thirst after righteousness. Your
desires after holiness, the yearnings of your
spirit will be satisfied; partly so in this life, with
many a secret, hidden token of God's favour and
presence; with joy and peace in believing;
satisfied completely in the bliss of that inheritance purchased for you by the Passion and
death of Christ. " I am that living Bread which
came down from Heaven ; if any man eat of this
bread, he shall live for ever." " Whosoever
drinketh of the water that I shall give him shall
never thirst; but the water that I shall give him
shall be in him a well of water springing up
into everlasting life."

Again. Jesus said unto them, "I am the
Bread of Life : he that cometh to Me shall
never hunger; and he that believeth on Me
shall never thirst." Inexhaustible is the fulness
of Christ. " Ye shall be filled."

As you stand on the margin of some noble
river, it is instructive to reflect, that although
it has been flowing for thousands of years,
watering the fields, slaking the thirst of a hundred generations, it yet shows no sign of waste
or diminution.   And when you watch the rising
sun as he shoots above the crest of the mountain, or in a sky draped with golden curtains
springs from his ocean bed, it is wonderful to
think that that sun has melted the snows of so
many Winters, and renewed the verdure of so
many Springs, and painted the flowers of so
many Summers, and ripened the golden har-
vests of so many Autumns, and yet shines with
floods of glorious light not less bright, not less
full.   These are but faint images which have
been used to describe the fulness that is in
Christ; fulness of pardon for the most guilty,
fulness of salvation to all who earnestly seek it.
" In Thy presence is fulness of joy, and at Thy
right hand are pleasures for evermore."

May we even now have experience of this
fulness; may our habitual life be one of such
earnest longing after holiness, that when we
go hence to be no more seen, when the last day,
and the last hour, and the last minute of our

earthly existence draws nigh, we may be enabled to say and feel in our last moments, in full assurance of faith, that which the Psalmist has recorded as his own experience and faith,—

" As for me, I will behold Thy face in righteousness : I shall be satisfied, when I awake, with Thy likeness."

SERMON XI.

PRAYER.

St. John xvi. 23, 24.

" Verily, verily, I say unto you, Whatsoever ye shall ask the Father in My Name, He will give it you.

" Hitherto have ye asked nothing in My Name: ask, and ye shall receive, that your joy may be full[1]."

.It has been remarked, and with much truth, that whenever our blessed Lord would declare some very important fact or doctrine, such as might be considered a fundamental. truth of Christianity, or a law of His spiritual kingdom, He invariably prefaced His declaration with the emphatic words 'Αμὴν, 'Αμὴν, which we translate "Verily, verily." If when you read the New Testament

---

[1] Gospel for Fifth Sunday after Easter.

yourselves, you will note the passages in which these reiterated words occur, you will see that they are always in connexion with some important Christian truth. In point of fact, it is no exaggeration to say that you might condense the distinctive teaching of Christianity in the few verses which are prefaced with these particles of speech, and draw up from them a succinct summary of those essential verities of the Christian creed, as distinct from Natural Religion, which we hold to be necessary to our salvation.

One or more instances out of many will suffice to confirm these remarks. The Pre-existence of Christ and His eternal Godhead[2] are thus declared : " Verily, verily, I say unto you, Before Abraham was, I am[3]." The descent of Christ into the grave[4] : " Verily, verily, I say unto you, Except a corn of wheat fall into the ground and die, it abideth alone ; but if it die, it bringeth forth much fruit[5]." The universal Resurrection and future judgment : " Verily, verily, the hour is coming, in the which all that are in the graves shall hear His Voice, and shall come forth ; they that have done good unto the resur-

---

[2] Compare Article II.   Exod iii. 14.
[3] John viii. 58.   [4] Article III.
[5] John xii. 24.

rection of life, and they that have done evil
unto the resurrection of damnation⁶." The
future glory of Christ in His Second Coming :
"Verily, verily, I say unto you, Hereafter ye
shall see Heaven open, and the angels of God as-
cending and descending upon the Son of Man⁷."
The necessity of the new birth as a condition
of future happiness; of union with Christ by
faith imaged under the symbol of Manna; of
belief in Him as essential to salvation; all these
laws and conditions of His spiritual kingdom are
prefaced with the same words.   And not to
quote more passages to the same purpose, shortly
before His Ascension to glory, when He would
comfort His disciples in their sorrow at the prospect of His near departure, when He would
encourage them to brave all the tribulation
through which they must pass for His sake, He
once more, in revealing to them the truth of His
mighty intercession for them at the Throne of
Grace, and for all prayerful Christians in all
ages, emphasizes His declaration concerning
Prayer, and thus seems to give it a prominent
place in the system of Christianity.

"Verily, verily, I say unto you, Whatsoever

---

⁶ John v. 28.   ⁷ John i. 51.

ye shall ask the Father in My Name, He will give it you."

In common, brethren, with all sentient creation, even with types and forms of organized structures much lower down in the scale of creation than man, we have certain Instincts indissolubly connected with our individual being and nature. Some are of opinion that even plants are possessed of Instincts. It is certain that they perform all the principal and important functions of animal life, such as assimilation, absorption, secretion. The sap is circulated throughout the plant as the blood circulates in our veins. The plant obeys the conditions of growth and decay. It would seem, moreover, to be endowed with Instincts. You must have often observed how it instinctively turns its opening petals to the blessed light of Heaven, place it where you will. " The sunflower turns to her God." Not a few open and close their petals with the rising and the setting sun. As the Christian poet writes—

> " *Go, sleep like closing flowers at night,*
> *And Heaven thy morn will bless* [8]*.*"

The shoots of the potato will find their way

---

[8] Keble's Christian Year. Fifteenth Sunday after Trinity.

in the dark cave or cellar, and penetrate as by an instinct through chink and crevice, upward and upward, until they reach the light of day. The roots of the vine, feeling their way, will spread themselves out far and wide in search of the cool spring and satisfying moisture. Most plants have the property of secreting certain substances, essential to the fabric of the plant, and which enter into its tissue. If you supply artificially the water in which the plant is placed with these substances, the plant as by an instinct secretes them; when you analyze the water which remains, you find these substances have been eliminated and withdrawn; and if you submit the petal of the plant to the microscope, on examination you find the siliceous deposit formed on the surface in definite crystals[*]. The Instinct of the brute creation, so much stronger for all the purposes of existence and self-preservation than that of Man, is familiar to us all, and might be abundantly shown in every department of zoology. The best definition, perhaps, that has ever been given of Instinct is that given by Paley. He defines it as "a propensity prior to experience and independent of instruction." By another

---

[*] The *Deutzia scabra*, the group of *Equisetaceæ*, most *Grasses*, and also *Rice*, afford familiar and beautiful examples.

and recent writer it is defined " by being opposed
to acquisition, education, or experience. We
might express it," he says, " as the *untaught*
ability to perform actions of all kinds. It is
part of the original mechanism apart from all
acquired faculties [1]."

Strictly analogous to these purely physical
instincts, part of our "original mechanism,"
are certain spiritual instincts, part of our
spiritual nature. Of these we may also say
that they are " prior to experience and independent of instruction." The idea, the recognition of a God would seem to be instinctive,
intuitive. The child who lisps with infant lips
those few syllables of morning and evening
prayer, the meaning of which it scarcely under-
stands, bends its little knees in instinctive ador-
ation of Him of Whom it is said, " In Heaven
their angels do always behold the face of My
Father, which is in Heaven." By degrees this
Instinct is educated, if I may so speak. We
are instructed in those truths relating to God
which as children we could not understand, which
we could not think out for ourselves, which are
matter of express and particular revelation. It
may so be that the soul, being a spark of

[1] Bain on the Senses and the Intellect, p. 261.

Divinity, is in itself the source and origin within us of this intuitive conception and recognition, even in our infancy, of the existence of a God. So, if we may judge from the prevalent feature of propitiatory sacrifice in all known forms of religious belief, even amongst the rude and untutored tribes, the necessity of the Atonement would seem to be an instinctive conviction and yearning of the human mind. A belief in the future, which as yet has no existence, and which cannot, therefore, in the strict sense of the word, be an object of our *knowledge,* is another of these instinctive convictions. It is confirmed by the inference the mind draws from observation of antecedent and consequent in the phenomena of Nature; it is established by the revelation of God's Holy Word [2].

Shall we not say that Prayer is an Instinct of our spiritual nature? Does not praying to God, seeking Him in and through Prayer, answer to the purely animal Instinct of Hunger and Thirst?

> " —— *The soul's sincere desire*
> *Uttered or unexpressed ;*
> *The motion of a hidden fire,*
> *That trembles in the breast.*"

[2] Brown, "Philosophy of Human Mind," p. 34.

Is not Prayer to our spiritual life, to its growth, activities, energies, what Hunger is, which impels us to labour for food; what Thirst is, which constrains us to satisfy the want of our physical nature? Might we not be content to rest our reply to the specious but fallacious argument of the Deist on this fact alone? The difficulties and objections that have been urged in connexion with Prayer, the contradictions it is urged Prayer involves, the inconsistencies it is charged with; these we must remember are of human and shortsighted reasoning. They are nowhere to be found throughout the length and breadth of Scripture, which never disguises the difficulties connected with our approach to God and our final salvation, but on the contrary frequently insists upon them. In Scripture it is always *assumed* that Prayer is a recognized means of approaching God. It is said, "Ask, and ye shall receive; seek, and ye shall find; knock, and it shall be opened unto you;" and there are many more passages of the same tenor. The Deist argues that all such things as are agreeable to the will of God must be accomplished, whether we pray or not; and, therefore, our prayers are useless, unless they be supposed to have a power of altering His Will.

Such an argument, if valid, strikes at the root of all religious belief. It might be equally applied to the inefficacy as well as uselessness of repentance, and to the doctrine of a mediator between God and Man. It is, however, urged that Prayer argues changeableness and mutability in Him "in Whom is no variableness, neither shadow of turning." So far, however, from arguing mutability in God, may not Prayer be, as we have every reason from the frequent exhortations respecting it to believe it to be—the very condition, the *sine quâ non*, in God's spiritual kingdom, by compliance with which God's purposes are fulfilled in and towards us? In the world of Nature certain conditions have to be fulfilled, by compliance with which we make a practical use of its phenomena. The phenomena exist, whether we apply them or not to the purposes of existence. How far they become ours; how far the mighty forces of the universe become subservient to the Arts and Sciences, to general or individual application, depends on our compliance with certain recognized conditions. And it is so also in the spiritual kingdom. "The unchangeableness of God," as it has been observed, "consists not in always acting in the same manner, however cases and circumstances may alter, but *in always doing what is right,* and in adapting His treatment of His intelligent creatures to the variations of their actions, characters, and dispositions. Prayer is not to be considered as a yielding to importunity, but as an instance of rectitude in suiting His dealings with us to our conduct[3]." We do not suppose that Prayer alters the will of God in any particular towards us, for this would be to regard Him as mutable; but we hold that there are certain conditions, on the performance of which the effects of His goodness to us are suspended; that there is something to be done by us before we can be proper objects of His bounty, or before it can be consistent with His divine government to grant us particular benefits. Before Prayer, we may be unworthy, the very act of prayer being in and of itself the very condition in our individual character which contributes to render us the proper objects of Divine regard, and the neglect of it being that which disqualifies us from receiving blessings. "This objection," says Paley[4], " admits of but one answer, viz. that it may be agreeable to

---

[3] Magee on the Atonement, note viii.
[4] Paley on the Duty and Efficacy of Prayer.

perfect wisdom to grant that to our prayers, which it would not have been agreeable to the same wisdom to have given us without praying for." "If prayer," writes another [b], "were not enjoined for the perfection, it would be permitted to the weakness of our nature. We should be betrayed into it, if we thought it sin; and pious ejaculations would escape our lips, though we were obliged to preface them with 'God forgive me for praying.' To those who press the objection, that we cannot see in what manner our prayers can be answered, consistently with the government of the world according to general laws, it may be sufficient to say, that prayer, being made almost an instinct of our nature, it cannot be supposed but that, like all other instincts, it has its use."

May we not fairly urge against all such dry, sceptical, and calculating reasoning as this, founded on only partial knowledge, that prayer being an instinct of our nature, has its use? Is it not so that the soul finds relief in the opportunity prayer affords of unburdening the mind and conscience? One is soothed and calmed down in this devotional exercise; to

[b] Mrs. Barbauld.

another, care is greatly lightened; trouble is rolled away as the stone from the door of the sepulchre; aching hearts are comforted; the feeble supported; the weak strengthened; the desponding encouraged; the faithful blessed. These are forms in which Prayer is answered and is of use, suited to individual cases and characters. This is matter of familiar experience. And is not Prayer to our spiritual life and health what the air we breathe is to our physical existence? So long as you inhale the surrounding air, and it is constantly supplied, so long, and so long only, you live. Death quickly ensues when we are deprived of air essential to existence. So there is no spiritual life apart from Prayer. What we, each one of us, now are, we are by prayer or by the neglect of prayer. If we have attained any measure of goodness; if we have resisted temptations; if we have any self-control; if we live with aspirations and desires beyond the common, ascribe it all to answered prayer. If sin still has dominion over you; if the power of some lusts is still uncrippled and unbroken; if there is no hungering and thirsting after righteousness; no conscious effort after holiness; no increased spiritual strength, ascribe it all, not to

s

God, but to neglected or unbelieving prayer.
Have you not sometimes seen two plants, the
one showing a mass of flowers which dazzles
the eye with their beauty, the other, fruitless
and flowerless, hangs its drooped and withered
leaves, and seems pining away in its sickness to
death?   Both are cuttings from one and the
same parent stock.   Both have taken root in the
same soil.   On both the sun shines with equal
warmth.   Yet one is vigorous and in health,
the other is languishing and ready to perish.
Whence the difference?   Not in the parent
tree; not in the common soil; not in the equal
temperature.   The one has been diligently and
frequently watered; the other has been overlooked and neglected.   It is so with ourselves.
What copious and refreshing moisture is to the
thirsty plant in summer heat and drought, such
is prayer, habitual prayer, daily prayer, believing
prayer, to our soul's vigour and growth.

> " *It is the Christian's vital breath,*
>   *The Christian's native air ;*
>   *His watchword at the gates of death—*
>   *He enters heaven with prayer.*"

Assuming, my brethren, that all we here
assembled are agreed to regard Prayer as a

necessity of our humanity; 'assuming that from
your childhood upwards, when you scarce understood the few words of prayer which were taught
you at a parent's lips, up to this present day,
you have always felt and acknowledged the
place which prayer holds in your spiritual life
and its exercises, the text suggests one or more
reflections of a practical nature to which I invite
your listening attention. I say of a practical
nature, for what subject enters so much into, is
so much concerned with our common, daily life,
as this, in which all devotion is briefly summed
up? What is more frequently urged upon us
throughout Scripture as something more than
mere duty, as the very highest privilege which
we in this our fallen condition can enjoy, being
the direct means of holding communion with
the Eternal Father?

In the first place, then, experience tells us
that a passage of Scripture such as my text
must not be read and accepted in its literality;
or rather, that it must be modified in its inter-
pretations. We must explain Scripture by
Scripture if we would understand it aright.
For we know, and doubtless this has been the
experience of many amongst yourselves, that
" whatsoever we ask for," all things for which

we pray are not always granted to us. For
years, and for long years, you have asked of
God some earthly blessing which He from year
to year has seen fit in His infinite wisdom to
deny you. You have knelt down day by day,
morning by morning, evening by evening, and
have laid before Him the strong desire, the
ardent longing, the secret wish, and day by day
no answer has come, no answer, at least, such
as you expected and desired. How is this?
Has God, for all these years, "covered Himself
with a cloud that your prayer might not pass
through [6]?"

Scripture elsewhere lays down this as one
of the conditions essential to prayer and to
answered prayer, "that if we ask any thing
according to His will, He heareth us." According to His will;—this is the limit, as it
were, imposed on our prayers. The instinct of
human nature must be guided by reason, it
must be corrected and overruled by the wisdom
of God. We ask blindly, on the impulse of
the moment; under excited feelings; we often
ask ignorantly and foolishly. We do not,
we cannot, see beyond the present moment.
The future, as God sees it, is hidden, yes,

[6] Lam. iii. 44.

wisely hidden from our short-sighted view. Who
of us can tell what to-morrow may bring forth;
what unlooked for event may occur to any one
of us to change the current of our whole life?
We do not know in our ignorance, we do not
see in our blindness, what would be good and
best for us. We pray for things which, if
granted, would prove a curse and not a blessing,
like the Israelites, who asked that God would give
them flesh to eat, "and while the flesh was yet
between their teeth, ere it was chewed, the
wrath of the Lord was kindled against the people, and the Lord smote the people with a very
great plague." How often, as we look back on
life, do we acknowledge that it was well our
prayer was not granted! How often have we
had reason to thank God that He, with loving
care and forethought, has denied us our request!
Some prayers are answered in judgment, some
are denied in mercy. Often God sends us the
very contrary to that for which we have so
earnestly prayed. We pray that He will take
away our anxieties, and He rather increases
them. We ask Him to remove some present
anguish, and He rather deepens our sorrow.
We ask Him for happiness and sunshine, He
sends us sadness and overshadowing clouds.

We ask for health, He sends us sickness; for comforts and wealth, He sends us hardness and straitened means. We ask Him to heal some one by whose sick bed we are anxiously watching, or to spare to us one dear to us as our own life; and He seems in that hour of intense anxiety and suspense to read all our prayers backwards.

Brethren, God has a distinct purpose in view with each one of us. His purpose is being carried out in various ways; with many it is carried out, and in part fulfilled through delayed and also through denied prayer. Our prayers are answered in harmony with His divine will and purpose. Answered, I say, because they are always answered, if not in the way we looked for and desired, yet in God's good way, and even by contraries. All good things for which we ask, all spiritual gifts and graces, all unearthly blessings, the pledged mercies of redemption, these His best gifts He will assuredly give you as you earnestly desire and importunately make request for them. All these things He will give you as He sees good for you; not always as you think good for yourself. He has His purpose, and that purpose is carried out in refusals as well as in granted petitions. For remember what the object of all true prayer is. It is not merely the obtaining of our own wishes, for this would often be to obtain a curse and not a blessing; but it is to bring our human will into submission to the Divine, supreme will. "The object of prayer," as it has been truly said, "is not the success of its petition, nor is its rejection a proof of failure." Christ prayed that the cup of bitterness might pass from Him. The answer to that prayer was this: "There appeared unto Him an angel, strengthening Him." Prayer does not change the outward universe; it does not alter the laws of Nature; it does not alter God. It is to teach us submission to the Divine will; it is to train and discipline us into obedience to and recognition of a higher will than our own, as we accept denials with resignation, and learn what that will is by the answers which God sends. And that prayer which does not succeed in moderating our wishes, in changing the passionate desire into still submission, the tremulous expectation into silent surrender, is no true prayer. "We should pray till prayer makes us forget our wish, and leave or merge it in God's will. The Divine Wisdom has given us prayer, not as a means whereby to obtain the good things of earth, but as a means whereby we may learn to do without them; not as a means whereby we may escape evil, but as a means whereby we become strong to meet it." When, therefore, you read such a passage as my text, bear in mind that our prayers, to be answered, must be in harmony and accordance with the Divine will, and that that will is declared as often in refusals as in granted petitions.

Remember also that as habitual prayer is the great secret of the spiritual life, so the secret of success in prayer is faith. We commit sins even when on our knees in prayer. When we pray, we have often to ask forgiveness for the unbelieving spirit in which we pray. Prayer is truest when there is most of instinct in it, and least of reason; when it does not coldly calculate probabilities and improbabilities, but when it is the instinctive utterance of our longing spirit. How often do we "ask amiss!" We kneel down, it is true; with our lips we utter so many words, but we do not pray *in faith;* we do not in our hearts *believe* that God will answer our prayers. When the answer comes we do not recognize it as God's reply, or we say, " How extraordinary this is," when what we have desired is granted, and events conspire, under God's ordering, to bring about that for which we prayed. Nor are we content and willing to *wait* for a reply, which will surely come, even though we have to wait for long and weary years. In our impatience, in the turbulence of our emotions, we forget the great truth that often our " strength is to sit still." How many have prayed from childhood, from lisping infancy to toothless, mumbling old age, and yet have never prayed. If our heart is not in our prayer; if we do not believe in the efficacy of prayer; if it is the cold, formal, routine petition, borrowed second-hand from devotional books; the thoughts of other men and not our own; expressive of another's necessities and not of ours; if it is not that Prayer which is the result of self-examination, and the waiting of our souls on Christ in simple, childlike faith, what wonder that no notice is taken of prayers such as these? What wonder if God does not answer a prayer which so dishonours Him? No, my brethren; say that the prayer of your heart comes back to you again and again like a stone; say that it never seems to penetrate beyond the four walls of your chamber, and never to reach the throne of grace, still, and still, and still pray. Whenever you approach God in prayer for yourself or for others, for your own spiritua. and temporal necessities, or for the spiritual and temporal welfare of one dear to you—as we are encouraged to pray for one another—go before God with an undoubting mind, remembering that the secret of success lies in this, "Let him ask *in faith*, nothing wavering." "The Lord is nigh unto all them that call upon Him; yea, all such as call upon Him *faithfully.*" "All things whatsoever ye shall ask in prayer *believing*, ye shall receive."

Remember also that over and above submitting your will to God's will; over and above childlike, trusting faith, your prayer, to be accepted, must be helped by the pleading of God's Holy Spirit, and presented to God's all-hearing ear, through the intercession our ascended Lord, Who is our Mediator and Advocate. Honour Christ in your prayers. Never pray, never conclude your prayers, however brief, without asking God to accept them for Christ's sake and merits. He knows us as perfect man. The mysterious knowledge of personal experience, of personal suffering in human flesh which He gained on earth, He has still in Heaven, even as He bears still the prints of the nails and the spear-gash in His wounded side. Even before the Eternal Throne, even there amidst all its inconceivable glories, its perfect peace, its unbroken tranquillity, He retains a perfect sense of our infirmities, of all the mystery of human sorrow which He learned on earth from the cradle to the Cross. It is out of this perfect knowledge and sympathy that He perpetually intercedes for us according to our trial and our day. Realize this truth for your encouragement, to stimulate you to perseverance, as a source of consolation and comfort in the hour of despondency, that " Whatsoever ye shall ask the Father in My Name, He will give it you."

And doubtless if you pray in this spirit, in this frame of mind, in submission to God's most holy will; in faith ; in humble reliance on the merits and intercession of our Lord Jesus Christ, you will often and often experience the full blessedness of prayer. In the reality of this promise, " Ask, and ye shall receive, that your joy may be full," you will have the desire of your heart, and if not always that, yet something better than you can either ask or think ; God's best and choicest blessings showered down upon your head in this your chequered life ; support throughout your earthly pilgrimage onward to the end ; peace of mind when you will need it in the prospect of death ; everlasting joy in that better world where prayer shall be turned into praise.

God is every day giving us fresh proofs for our encouragement of the sustaining power of Prayer; of what it does, and can do under the heaviest of earthly trials; in the darker hours of life; under circumstances the most calculated to depress us; even in the very face of a painful and agonizing death. Must it not prove a source of consolation to those at home to whom he was dear; to a parent, wife, child, sister, or friend who loved him dearly and well, to know that the [7] missionary who, risking his life in the cause of Christ, has recently met with a most cruel and agonizing death at the hands of fanatics, could meet such a death with composure, when all hope of rescue was cut off? What greater proof can we desire of the sustaining power of believing prayer, to work miracles of sustaining strength and resignation; what plainer evidence of the effectual intercession of Christ for His faithful servants, and of the reality of IIis consoling presence than is given us in those few words which simply sum up the intelligence which has reached this country of that missionary's painful death, " He died calmly, praying; he died calmly, praying."

[7] Alluding to the death of Rev. M. Volkner at the hands of the Pai Mariri fanatics at Opotiki, New Zealand.

SERMON XII.

DEUT. xxxii. 29.

*" O that they were wise, that they understood this,
that they would consider their latter end !"*

MY brethren, God, in His mysterious dealings,
has been pleased to visit our country with what,
without exaggeration, may be regarded as a
national calamity. The universal manifestation of sorrow which the melancholy event has
called forth, not only on the part of this great
nation, but abroad, and wheresoever the sad
tidings has reached, evidences how great, how
wide-felt, how irreparable is the loss which we
have sustained in the death of the lamented
Prince Consort.

So great has been the shock, so sudden, so
unexpected, that we scarce can realize the melancholy fact. Sadness possesses every mind

capable of feeling. Every heart is touched
with tenderest sympathy for our bereaved and
widowed Queen. Her loss is ours. " We
shared her joy, and will not be denied to share
her grief." If tears and pity could recall the
dead, if the sad tribute of a nation's sorrow
could restore to life him whose sun has so early
set, this tribute of sympathy had not been withheld, but every where paid with loyal, genuine,
heartfelt sincerity.

The calamity which has befallen us is one of
no ordinary kind. Death, at any time an occasion of mourning, is, however, not rarely attended
with circumstances which mitigate our grief or
reconcile us to our loss. Sometimes it is the
natural, expected termination to a life full of
years—the last day in the autumn of man's
short-lived existence here. Often a long and
lingering illness gradually and mercifully prepares the mind for the fatal issue, and by long
anticipation we become familiarized with the
prospect of a separation from those we love.

There are even circumstances under which
Death is looked forward to as a happy release
from suffering; when the heart-broken and
despairing child of adversity longs for the undis-
turbed quiet of the grave, " where the wicked

cease from troubling, and the weary are at rest."
Sometimes men attain that age when they may
be said to have outlived their generation. Life
has no great or further interest for them. They
have followed to their last resting-place the
companions of their youth. They have shed
tears over the grave of the friends of their manhood. There are but few old familiar faces left.
They are isolated from the crowd of human
beings around them by having nothing of pursuit or interest in common. They derive enjoyment no more from what once was to them a
source of pleasure. They can no longer extract
from the scenes of life the freshness which youth
and health imparted to them. Like the last
withered leaf which clings tenaciously to the
bough rudely shaken by the wind, but which the
next fitful gust will violently loosen from its
hold, so they remain for a while, the last remnant
of a departed generation, ready to fall amongst
those already shed and fallen. The chronic
disease, diminished power of exertion, general
prostration of strength, confinement in great
measure to one spot, these render the more aged
of our fellow-men unequal to any sustained
effort of mind or body, and preclude them
from taking a part in those more active occu-

pations which give to Life its interest and meaning. "Their strength is but labour and sorrow." Hence the void their death creates is scarcely noticed beyond the immediate circle of their relatives or acquaintance.

Again, the vast majority of men enjoy a necessarily limited sphere of usefulness. The place they occupy in the social scale is not of that prominence which gives the importance that belongs to a more elevated position or superior rank. Their existence is not of the same moment to the general well-being of the community. Their decease does not excite more than a local and personal regret.

It does, however, occasionally happen that Death, in its ever-busy, ruthless ravages, selects one out of the midst of the mass, whose selection excites general consternation, concern, and sorrow. "Spare him yet a little longer!" we say involuntarily. "Society requires his presence. His talents, his wisdom, his counsel are indispensable to us. We have confidence in his judgment in a season of national disquietude. The void his subtraction will create cannot easily be filled up. We look in vain for another who shall supply his place; who shall be to us in all respects what he has been." Those of you who have lived the longest will remember occasions when feelings such as these have been experienced and expressed.

May we not say with truth, that such a selection has recently been made? Who could have foreseen it? Such a void is created. Who was prepared for it? Such an one is gone from the midst of us. The place knoweth him no more. That name, so familiar to every man, is now but a name. That mind, ever occupied with intellectual pursuits, and intent on philanthropic schemes, has for ever quitted this sphere of exercise. The civilized world has lost in him one who was an active promoter of every thing calculated to elevate and improve the human race. Over his untimely grave are shed the scalding tears of a widowed Queen—of fatherless children. Who is there who grieves not at this unlooked-for bereavement to her, who must henceforth bear alone and undivided the anxieties and responsibilities of her exalted station? Who of us is not deeply concerned at the loss of one who made our people's welfare his constant study?

Not in a ripe old age, but in the prime and heyday of life has he passed away. Not with the full corn in the ear, ready for the autumn harvest, but in the summer of his manhood the

T

Reaper came. Not like some withered fruitless tree, whose vitality is spent and gone, but as the flower of the field, in full and healthy bloom, the Angel's sickle has mowed him down. No lingering sickness had prepared us for his loss, nor made him wish for death. A few days' fever, and his spirit fled! His mind was not saddened by the retrospect of life, or by the memory of outlived, departed friends. To-morrow, the companions of his youth will be the pall-bearers to his grave. The interests of life had not ceased for him. His was that age when those interests as Husband, Father, Counsellor, Friend, are most and greatest. He died surrounded by those who loved him best, in the enjoyment of every thing that makes Life dear and coveted. His were exalted rank as the husband of a devoted Queen, and high position with its influence and opportunities of usefulness. Wealth, with its many advantages, was at his command. His was a cultivated mind, in full possession of its every faculty. He had a refined taste, which gave an impulse and encouragement to Art and Science. He was distinguished in an eminent degree for those moral qualities and Christian virtues which adorn the private character, and lend a lustre of their own to rank and

station. How inestimable the value of these in
the parent of the Prince, on whose religious education and moral training our national well-being
will so largely depend ! He possessed a physical
constitution which to the outward eye gave promise of yet many years of usefulness to his
adopted country, and in which his various talents
might continue to be exercised for the general
good. If in his lifetime men were slow to accord
him the due meed of praise, and to acknowledge
his merits, in his death he obtains what in life
was withheld. Now that he is gone, all unite
in paying to his memory the long arrear of gratitude. Death consecrates such as these[1]. The
civilized world will feel the loss of one whose
life and example contributed to civilization;
Society, the void created by his departure hence.
Art regrets in him its warmest patron ; Science,
a diligent disciple and friend. The statesman
will want his judicious counsel, our country his
mature and sober judgment. To our Queen the
loss of such a husband is irreparable. Sons and
daughters mourn the parent, who sought to train
them in the fear of God, and to fit them for the
grave responsibilities which belong to Princes.

[1] "Mors illos consecrat, quorum exitum et qui timent
audant."

If tempted to call his death untimely, yet he is to be envied in his death. He who lives well, lives long. " He being made perfect in a short time, fulfilled a long time." To him we may with truth apply the maxim of one of old :— " Honourable age is not that which standeth in length of time, nor that is measured by years ; but wisdom is the grey hairs unto men, and an unspotted life is old age [2]."

An event, my brethren, of this solemn character, has its emphatic, its impressive teaching. The all-absorbing topic of conversation, it arrests the thoughts of even the most unthinking. It is well, therefore, to turn it to some good account, while still fresh in the memory ; before the impression it has created be weakened and deadened, or altogether effaced by the ever new and changing succession of ideas, which displace one another in the mind, inseparable from the occupations of our every-day life.

As Christians, as fellow-men, we have each a solemn interest in his death. It has its lesson for survivors, who, like him, are mortal, dying men. Whilst, therefore, your sorrow still is fresh, and this city, as we walk its streets, is as

---

[2] Wisdom of Solomon, cap. iv. ver. 8, 9.

if in every house there were one dead; whilst we
are wearing the sober garment of mourning, and
the last funeral rites have yet to be performed;
before his remains be borne to their last resting-
place, and the tomb be sealed, seek we to apply
to our own individual hearts the lesson which
his mournful death should teach us, even the
same which is implied in my text, " O that
they were wise, that they understood this, that
they would consider their latter end! "

There is no truth with which we are more
familiar than this, " *It is appointed unto men once
to die.*" There is no one to which, considering
the certainty of the fact, we are more insensible.
We do not habitually bear it in mind. We do
not even make the mental effort to realize from
time to time the terminal goal in the highway
of Life. The thought of dissolution is abhor-
rent to the mind. It demands of us no small
resolution, vividly, and with composure, to
contemplate the closing scene of our earthly
history, with all the affecting circumstance
which attends the deathbed. Yet Death is an
event of the most ordinary frequent occurrence.
It takes place next door to us; in the circle
of our friends, in the very heart of our families.
It summons those with whom we were but

yesterday conversing. Its shadow is ever cast athwart our path. In this city alone, the weekly average of deaths is upwards of one thousand. But this notorious fact does not sensibly affect us. It does not powerfully arrest our thoughts, or give rise to any solemn reflection. We regard this weekly mortality as a statistical fact. So far from being impressed by it, we consider it as a matter of course, that in so vast a population, there should be a proportionate number of deaths. How rarely do we reflect on the possibility of our own being added to that number! that our name may occur in the next week's register of mortality!

Nothing is more strange, I will not say unaccountable, than this insensibility. Strange, because Life and Death are, under various aspects, continually before us. They are the most familiar of mysteries. Deep below the earth's crust in fossil remains, and in the petrified relics of extinct species, we discover evidence of the presence of Death. It is an essential feature of the past and present system of organized nature. It must have entered into the plan of Creation in the Divine mind originally, so universal is the law of decay and dissolution. Generation after generation has passed away from off the face of the earth since man was first created. There has been an incessant, unvarying departure of old, and succession of new forms of Life. The world around us may be regarded as one vast sepulchre, in which myriads upon myriads of the human race lie entombed. Earth, air, and water hold in solution the constituent and kindred elements of men and women, who were once as we are now, living sentient beings. Nature around us in her changing seasons, bears eloquent testimony to the constant operation of this same law. The decay of Autumn follows in due course on the verdure of Spring and the Summer foliage. The torpor of Winter succeeds to Autumn. The returning Spring is almost like creation out of chaos, like life from a state of death.

Not only is this true of the outer world, in the vegetable kingdom; it is equally true of ourselves. As soon as we are born we begin to die. The seeds of Death are already there. The predisposing causes, which will eventually bring about the extinction of Life, are latent in the system. These may for a time be kept in check, counterbalanced by agencies conducive to the support of animal life, but ultimately they will preponderate with fatal power. The processes of Life induce changes in the structure which gradually impede its functions. The operations of the complex and delicate machinery are limited by an irresistible law of nature. Wherever there is vital energy and organization, Death is inevitable. Vital energy becomes exhausted, and the functions necessarily cease. Repair and Waste are the opposite conditions of existence. These are never identical, never nicely balanced, otherwise Life could never terminate save by some accident, never by old age. Obediently to certain physical laws, Life cannot be prolonged beyond a certain period. It must come to an end. Death is really and truly the inevitable result of the activity of Life. The spirit must return to the God who gave it.

Apart from, or rather in confirmation of these confessed facts, what is our own experience? Of what does our own observation satisfy us? Is it not of this, that in the midst of life we are in death? It is calculated that with every moment one human being passes out of the world. Death observes no fixed rule. It exercises no discretion in the choice of its victims. It enters the palaces of kings with the same fatal step as into the hovel of the pauper. It lays its icy hand on the person of the Sovereign, as surely as on the meanest subject in his realms. No power on earth can wrest the doomed from its cruel grasp. It baffles all who would arrest the progress of the insidious disease. The most consummate skill cannot fan the expiring flame into warmth and vigour, or bid the ebbing tide of life to flow back and return. Sometimes it comes with ominous symptoms of its nearness. The hectic flush, the deadly pallor, the wasting strength, herald its approach. Sometimes it overtakes men suddenly, with no premonition or warning. It spares neither age nor sex. The strong are struck down at a stroke. The infant is taken out of the mother's arms relentlessly. Youth in its bloom, manhood in its prime, succumb to the inexorable decree. They who promised themselves many years, find their life come abruptly to its close. The old man not unfrequently follows his children to their early grave.

In the midst of all this we live! We occupy the abodes which others, now no more, have occupied. We assemble ourselves in places of resort, where thousands before us were wont to assemble. We congregate in this House, where voices, now hushed in silence, have prayed and sung praises to God. The funeral procession passes us daily in the streets almost unnoticed. We are surrounded at every moment by harmful agencies and instruments of death ; by "the pestilence that walketh in darkness, and the sickness that destroyeth in the noon-day." Any one of a thousand fatal things, might in a moment extinguish the spark within us. The fever of a few days may hurry the healthiest of us out of this land of mortality. The cold of a few weeks may settle into some lingering and irrecoverable disease. The stroke of lightning may arrest the current of life in a twinkling. A slight fall may precipitate us into eternity. Exposure to rain, a gust of wind, a sudden chill, the slightest accident, may lay us on the bed of our last sickness, from which we are never more to rise. " Every hour men must have been aware that very slight changes in the external conditions rendered the manifestation of life impossible. A little more carbonic acid, or a little less oxygen, a little more heat or cold, a little less pressure of the atmosphere, a deficiency of water or of food, suffices to extinguish life, as a lamp is extinguished when the oil disappears [3]."

[3] Lewes, "Physiology of Common Life," cap. xiii. § 5.

And yet in the presence of all these facts, with all our experience of the uncertainty of life, and notwithstanding this multitude of harmful agencies, who of us thinks of his own death? Who does not soon recover his customary tenor of feeling, when he has been momentarily impressed? Who entertains the unwelcome truth in his mind? Do we not secretly promise to ourselves a prolongation of life, and say, " Soul, thou hast much goods laid up for many years; take thine case, eat, drink, and be merry?" Are we not in the habit of forming plans which project into the future, and with as much anticipating confidence of their being successfully prosecuted to completion, as if there were nothing whatever which could interrupt them? Do we not often calculate upon our being alive one, five, ten years hence, and speak of what we shall be, and of what we shall do then, not as men infallibly appointed to die should speak, but in terms of assurance, which prove that this stupendous reality is not a matter of serious, thoughtful contemplation? How shall we account for this? for so it is.

In endeavouring to account for this baneful insensibility to Death, some means may be suggested by which to overcome it. If we can discover the causes which operate so prejudicially against sober and serious meditation, we shall, at least, have made some progress towards bringing about a more healthy state of feeling on the subject.

If the mind were to dwell continually on the prospect of Death, the prospect would become so overpowering, as to arrest the whole economy of the world. Every thing would come to a stand-still. God, in His infinite wisdom, has implanted in our moral constitution a counteractive principle, which shall so limit this influence, that it shall not be inconsistent with our present state of being. Too habitual reflection on a subject, ordinarily associated with so much that is depressing, would induce a morbid condition of the mind, unfitting us for an energetic discharge of the duties of every-day life. But then, this is widely different from altogether ridding ourselves of the salutary influence, which occasional reflection on Death should exercise in every well-regulated mind.

Again, this insensibility may be in a great measure attributed to the fact that, to quote Bishop Butler's words, " from our very faculties of habits, passive impressions, by being repeated, grow weaker. Thoughts, by often passing through the mind, are felt less sensibly; being accustomed to danger begets intrepidity, i. e. lessens fear; to distress, lessens the passion of pity; to instances of others' mortality, lessens the sensible apprehension of our own[4]." The very fact of our familiarity with Death, tends to divest it of much of its solemnity. Were it to occur more rarely, say once in the year, or with the startling circumstance of last week, it would, in all probability, excite, as it did then, more general attention.

The fact of its certainty and universality is also to be reckoned amongst the causes which tend to withdraw our thoughts from a due contemplation of Death. If there were any doubt about it, whether it would or would not be, then there would be all the excitement of anxious suspense. But where the matter is removed beyond the region of doubt, this excitement subsides into a kind of dull fatalism.

So, again, its universality leaves no room for inquisitive wondering as to who is, and who is not to die; nor does it admit of that intense interest, which would be awakened, were a limited number of the race pronounced to be mortal.

[4] Butler's Analogy, cap. v. On a State of Moral Discipline.

Not to dwell upon the impossibility of forming any definite or distinct idea of our future existence, and the natural indisposition of the mind, surrounded as it is with objects of sense, to occupy itself with any, of which it must have a less vivid idea, there are other causes more common, more guilty, less excusable, than those above mentioned. ·

One is this: presuming upon a continuance of life. We find ourselves spared from day to day, from year to year. Others indeed are taken, but we are still here—are left. In imagination, the prospect of our life coming to a close is indefinitely remote. Each day that passes over our heads, instead of being regarded as one nearer to the last, only confirms us the more in our supposed tenure of life. We accustom ourselves to consider the last day as so distant, that it loses much of its dread importance, and thus diminished in significance, has little or no power to compel us to serious concern.

There is this also, the most prevailing and influential of all causes, viz. our real, strong attachment to the world; our intense love, not only of Life—that is natural—but of its pursuits, society, amusements, pleasures, possessions, friendships.

These absorb our thoughts, these preoccupy the
mind. The inner, higher, spiritual life, is kept
in check by these, is almost entirely lost sight
of. We form attachments which bind us by the
strong cords of affection to our fellow-creatures.
We acquire wealth, and surround ourselves with
every thing that can minister to the gratification
of our senses. The most innocent enjoyments
and pleasures possess an attraction of their own.
Hence we fly from a contemplation of our mortality. We shut out the darkening thought
that the strongest ties of affection will be rudely
sundered ; that the world will cease to have any
enjoyment for us; that the wealthiest " shall
carry nothing away with him when he dieth,
neither shall his pomp follow him." Riveted to
present objects of sense, deceived by the flatter-
ing aspect Life assumes, proud of our acquisi-
tions and powers, the mind is averse to the
thought of Eternity, of appearing before God,
of final judgment. Gloomy is the preacher who
would divert our thoughts from this changeful
world, and remind us of its transient nature ;
full of melancholy the voice which cries, " All
flesh is grass, and all the glory of man as the
flower of grass ;" too depressing that view of
Life which represents it as " a vapour which

appeareth for a little time and then vanisheth away." The amusing volume, the hasty re-course to some diverting occupation or cheerful society, which may give a new current to our thoughts, lest this one dreadful thought should influence and overpower us,—are we strangers to these expedients? Must we not confess to frequent, systematic endeavours to expel the intrusive reflection? Have they not been often only too successful?

And yet, my brethren, is this true wisdom? Is all this of which I have been speaking, con-sistent with the idea of our probationary state, and with the momentous interests of the undying soul? Does such an habitual insensibility to the mightiest event which yet awaits us, conduce to a healthy condition of the mind? Does it not necessarily tend to suppress within us those very emotions, and to discourage that anxious solicitude for the soul's eternal safety, which the certainty of our death should rather excite and suggest?

Is all this dread of death, and aversion to contemplate it, consistent with a firm belief in the joys of the unseen world, and of the better life to come? Does it not, on the contrary, argue a want of strong and real faith in the fundamental truths of religion, in Christ's victory over death, in the power of His Resurrection? Does it not imply that, whatever we may say, we are not fully and inwardly persuaded "that to depart and be with Christ is far better?" Is it not the most practical proof we can give that we still want, and that we still must, each man for himself, pray for the gift of the everlasting Spirit to quicken our unbelieving hearts, to give us a true and saving faith, to excite within us higher and holier aspirations? Is not the great incentive to a pure and holy life, the prospect of seeing God face to face, and being "for ever with the Lord" thus taken away?

And what can more effectually interfere with a due preparation for death, than indifference to death itself? How shall the great purposes of Life be ever carried out and realized, if now, in this accepted time, and in this the day of salvation with all its golden opportunities, we postpone to some indefinite period, or altogether neglect, the great work of preparation, until, alas! it be too late; until the Messenger of death brings to our door the awful summons which we cannot but obey, and which may find us unprepared to die?

My brethren, my brethren, the subject is in itself so solemn, there is so much calculated to

U

fasten it to-day on the mind of the most thoughtless, it is invested with such sorrowful and unusual
interest, that you can scarcely help putting to
yourself the question suggested by these remarks, " *Am I myself prepared to die ?* "

These are old, trite, time-worn truths.   But
do I realize them as I should?   Do I live constantly in view of them?   Have they a distinct,
real, sensible influence over me?   I have been
speaking to you this morning not of a probability, but of a certainty.   I have not been
endeavouring throughout this discourse to work
upon your imagination through some fictitious
supposition of an event which shall never take
place.   I have reminded you of a simple, sober
reality.   Year by year, week by week, day by
day, hour by hour, we silently approach nearer
to the end.   Since we entered those doors this
morning some have passed, and we have been
passing away.   We cannot stand by the stream
and watch it as it flows.   We are ourselves borne
down with it until it reaches that point where
its waters rush into and mingle with the boundless seas.

Are you living each day of your life as if it
might be your last?   Are you repenting truly
for your sins past, and resolving, through God's

help, never wilfully, consciously, and against
the voice of conscience, to offend Him? Are
you striving with all your soul and strength
against those lesser sins of infirmity which beset
even the holiest in the daily walk of life? Is
that daily life, notwithstanding all its home
cares, domestic duties, and lawful occupations,
one of a consistent walk with God, and as becometh the Gospel of Christ? Of what nature
are your customary prayers? Are they only for
temporal blessings, for prosperity, for success,
for honour, for advancement? Do you ask for
nothing more? Do you supplicate for the Spirit
of the living God, that He may be with you
throughout the day, to put into your heart good
desires, and to preserve you from falling into sin?
Do you seek for increased faith, for an abiding
union with Christ, and for all those spiritual
gifts and graces which adorn the soul, and make
us meet for the inheritance of the saints in light?
When you rise in the morning to the light and life
of another day, do you kneel down in some secret
place, and earnestly ask God, for Christ's sake,
to enable you to go forth upon it, and to discharge your several duties with a single eye to
His glory, and to live in it as one who must
shortly give up his account?

And again, ere you lie down to sleep, "so like to death that no good man will trust himself to it without his prayers," do you first humbly implore forgiveness, through Jesus Christ, for every sin that you may have committed, of ignorance, infirmity, omission, or presumption ? And if, my brother, you are conscious of some one habitual sin, or some one habit of life which the still small voice of your conscience emphatically reproves, are you endeavouring so completely to break away from it, and rid yourself of it, that, should the same temptation again present itself, it would have no chance of success ?

Do I speak to any whom the prospect of Death alarms? " The peace of God, which passeth all understanding, shall keep your heart and mind through Christ Jesus." Christ has overcome Death. He has robbed it for ever of its sting. If you are His, Death can have no power over you. It is the door through which all who die in the faith of Christ pass on to their Eternal Home. He who has redeemed you by His precious blood from that more dreadful, the second death, will redeem you from the grave. If you are His in life, He will say to your trembling spirit, in that solemn hour when the dark shadows of the valley fall thickest around us, and the rolling stream of the river of death threatens to overwhelm the soul, *" It is I, be not afraid ! "* Your remains committed to the earth with words of hope shall be safe in the Omnipotence of His keeping. True, we must return to the kindred dust; but the same God who created us can recreate us at His will. Though the conditions of our future being are unknown, and our remains must share in the general dissolution, yet we know in Whom we have believed. The grass may grow over our graves, the letters upon the tombstone, effaced by the hand of time, may have ceased to record the brief story of our life, but the imperishable soul shall survive our memory. And though in process of time no trace of us shall be left, and the elements, out of which this material fabric is formed, shall be scattered to the four winds of heaven, still not one soul that has taken refuge in Christ shall ever perish, but shall be found in Him in the day of His appearing. *" When Christ, who is our life, shall appear, then shall ye also appear with Him in glory."*

Thoughts such as these, solemn, consoling, sustaining, should be ours on this day. I have spoken to you with earnestness—who could be otherwise than earnest? Be earnest yourselves. If the sad event which we so deeply deplore has impressed you, seek to make those impressions permanent and influential. Lay we to heart, be we young or old, the solemn teaching of Death. This morning, in a few moments' silent prayer, pray we that we may live in a state of constant preparation for Death. To-morrow, when the funeral bells shall be heard tolling for the dead, when the remains of the husband of our beloved Sovereign shall be borne with hushed voice and mournful feet, and with weeping eyes to the grave, bear we in mind that our last hour must also come; and let this practical reflection on the great uncertainty of Life, and the inevitable certainty of Death, be ours,

"O that they were wise, that they understood this, that they would consider their latter end!"

THE END.

GILBERT AND RIVINGTON, PRINTERS, ST. JOHN'S SQUARE.

BOOKS LATELY PUBLISHED.

HOUSEHOLD THEOLOGY; a Handbook of
Religious Information. By the Rev. J. H. BLUNT,
Author of " Directorium Pastorale." Small 8vo. 6s.

CONTENTS :—1. The Bible—2. The Prayer Book—3. The
Church—4. Table of Dates—5. Ministerial Offices—6. Divine
Worship—7. The Creeds—8. Summary of Christian Doctrine
—9. Early Christian Writers—10. Heresies and Sects—11.
The Church Kalendar—12. Explanation of Terms. With an
Index.

The NEW TESTAMENT for ENGLISH
READERS : containing the Authorized Version, with a
revised English Text ; Marginal References ; and a Critical
and Explanatory Commentary. By HENRY ALFORD,
D.D., Dean of Canterbury. In Two large Volumes, 8vo.

Already published,

Vol. I., Part I., containing the first three Gospels, with a Map
of the Journeyings of our Lord, 12s.

Part II., containing St. John and the Acts, and completing
the first volume, 10s. 6d.

Vol. II., Part I., containing the Epistles of St. Paul, with a
Map, 16s.

A BOOK of FAMILY PRAYER. By WAL-
TER FARQUHAR HOOK, D.D., Dean of Chichester.
Seventh Edition, revised and enlarged. 18mo. 2s.

SHORT DEVOTIONAL FORMS, compiled to meet the Exigencies of a Busy Life. By EDWARD MEYRICK GOULBURN, D.D. New Edition, elegantly printed in square 16mo. 1*s.* 6*d.*

HYMNS from the **GERMAN**; translated by FRANCES ELIZABETH COX. With the Originals in German by Gerhard, Luther, Angelus, Wülffer, and others. Second Edition, revised and enlarged; elegantly printed in small 8vo. 5*s.*

A COMMENTARY on the **LORD'S PRAYER,** Practical and Exegetical. By the Rev. WILLIAM DENTON, M.A., Incumbent of St. Bartholomew's, Cripplegate. Small 8vo. 5*s.*

The **PUBLIC SCHOOLS CALENDAR** for 1865. Edited by a Graduate of the University of Oxford. Small 8vo. 6*s.*

*** This Work is intended to furnish Annually an account of the Foundations and Endowments of the Schools; of the Course of Study and Discipline; Scholarships and Exhibitions; Fees, and other Expenses; School Prizes and University Honours; Recreations and Vacations; Religious Instruction; and other Useful Information.

The **LONDON DIOCESE BOOK** for 1865: containing an account of the See and the succession of its Bishops; of St. Paul's Cathedral, Westminster Abbey, and the Chapels Royal; of the Rural Deaneries, and Foreign Chaplaincies; with other useful information. Under the sanction of the Lord Bishop of London. By JOHN HASSARD, Private Secretary to the Bishop. *Second Edition.* Crown 8vo. 2*s.* 6*d.*

RIVINGTONS;

LONDON, OXFORD, AND CAMBRIDGE.

A

SELECT LIST OF WORKS

PUBLISHED BY

MESSRS. RIVINGTON,

WATERLOO PLACE, PALL MALL, LONDON;

HIGH STREET, OXFORD;

AND TRINITY STREET, CAMBRIDGE.

Adams's (Rev. W.) The Shadow of the Cross; an Allegory.
A New Edition, elegantly printed in crown 8vo., with Illustrations.
3s. 6d. in extra cloth, gilt edges.

The Shadow of the Cross; an Allegory.

The Distant Hills; an Allegory.

The Old Man's Home; an Allegorical Tale.

The King's Messengers; an Allegory.
These four works are printed uniformly in 18mo., with Engravings,
price 9d. each in paper covers, or 1s. in limp cloth.

A Collected Edition of the Four Allegories, with
Memoir and Portrait of the Author: elegantly printed in crown 8vo.
9s. in cloth, or 14s. in morocco.

An Illustrated Edition of the above Sacred Allegories,
with numerous Engravings on Wood from Original Designs by C. W.
Cope, R.A., J. C. Horsley, A.R.A., Samuel Palmer, Birket Forster,
and George E. Hicks. Small 4to. 21s. in extra cloth, or 36s. in antique
morocco.

Adams's (Rev. W.) The Warnings of the Holy Week; being
a Course of Parochial Lectures for the Week before Easter, and the Easter
Festivals. Fifth Edition. Small 8vo. 4s. 6d.

A

Ainger's (Rev. T.) Practical Sermons. Small 8vo. 6s.

Ainger's (Rev. T.) Last Sermons: with a Memoir of the
Author prefixed. Small 8vo. 5s.

A Kempis, Of the Imitation of Christ. A carefully revised
translation; elegantly printed by Whittingham, in small 8vo, price 5s.
in antique cloth.

Alford's (Dean) Greek Testament; with a critically revised
Text: a Digest of Various Readings: Marginal References to Verbal and
Idiomatic Usage. Prolegomena: and a copious Critical and Exegetical
Commentary in English. In 4 vols. 8vo. 5l. 2s.

Or, separately,

Vol. I.—The Four Gospels. Fifth Edition. 28s.
Vol. II.—Acts to II. Corinthians. Fourth Edition. 24s.
Vol. III.—Galatians to Philemon. Third Edition. 18s.
Vol. IV.—Hebrews to Revelation. Second Edition. 32s.
The Fourth Volume may still be had in Two Parts.

Alford's (Dean) New Testament for English Readers:
containing the Authorized Version, with a revised English Text;
Marginal References; and a Critical and Explanatory Commentary.
In Two large Volumes, 8vo.

Already published,

Vol. I., Part 1, containing the first three Gospels, with a Map of the
Journeyings of our Lord, 12s.
Part 2. containing St. John and the Acts, and completing the first
volume, 10s. 6d.
Vol. II., Part 1, containing the Epistles of St. Paul, with a Map. 16s.

Alford's (Dean) Sermons on Christian Doctrine, preached in
Canterbury Cathedral, on the Afternoons of the Sundays in the year
1861-62. Second Edition. Crown 8vo. 7s. 6d.

Alford's (Dean) Sermons preached at Quebec Chapel, 1854
to 1857. In Seven Volumes, small 8vo. 2l. 1s.

Sold separately as follows:—

Vols. I. and II. (A course for the Year.) Second Edition. 12s. 6d.
Vol. III. (On Practical Subjects.) 7s. 6d.
Vol. IV. (On Divine Love.) Third Edition. 5s.
Vol. V. (On Christian Practice.) Second Edition. 5s.
Vol. VI. (On the Person and Office of Christ.) 5s.
Vol. VII. (Concluding Series.) 6s.

Anderson's (Hon. Mrs.) Practical Religion exemplified, by
Letters and Passages from the Life of the late Rev. Robert Anderson, of
Brighton. Sixth Edition. Small 8vo. 4s.

Annual Register; a Review of Public Events at Home and
Abroad, for the Years 1863 and 1864; being the First and Second Volumes
of an improved Series. 8vo. 18s. each.

Arnold's School Series (see page 18).

Arnold's (Rev. T. K.) Sermons preached in a Country
Village. Post 8vo. 5s. 6d.

Arnold's (Rev. Dr. T.) History of Rome, from the Earliest
Period to the End of the Second Punic War. New Edition. 3 vols. 8vo. 36s.

Arnold's (Rev. Dr. T.) History of the later Roman Com-
monwealth, from the End of the Second Punic War to the Death of Julius
Cæsar, with the Reign of Augustus, and a Life of Trajan. New Edition.
2 vols. 8vo. 24s.

Articles (The) of the Christian Faith, considered in reference
to the Duties and Privileges of Christ's Church Militant here on Earth.
Small 8vo. 3s. 6d.

Beaven's (Rev. Dr.) Questions on Scripture History. Fourth
Edition, revised. 18mo. 2s.

Beaven's (Rev. Dr.) Help to Catechising; for the use of
Clergymen, Schools, and Private Families. New Edition. 18mo. 2s.

Bethell's (Bishop) General View of the Doctrine of Regeneration in Baptism. Fifth Edition. 8vo. 9s.

Bickersteth's (Archdeacon) Questions illustrating the Thirty-
nine Articles of the Church of England: with Proofs from Scripture and
the Primitive Church. Fifth Edition. 12mo. 3s. 6d.

Bickersteth's (Archdeacon) Catechetical Exercises on the
Apostles' Creed; chiefly drawn from the Exposition of Bishop Pearson.
New Edition. 18mo. 2s.

Blunt's (Rev. J. H.) Directorium Pastorale: the Principles
and Practice of Pastoral Work in the Church of England. Crown 8vo. 9s.
   This work has been written with the object of providing for Theological
students and the younger Clergy a Practical Manual on the subject of
which it treats.
   Contents:—Chap. I. The nature of the Pastoral Office.—Chap. II.
The relation of the Pastor to God —Chap. III. The relation of the Pastor
to his flock.—Chap. IV. The ministry of God's Word.—Chap. V. The
ministry of the Sacraments, &c.—Chap. VI. The Visitation of the Sick.—
Chap. VII. Pastoral converse.— Chap. VIII. Private Instruction.—Chap.
IX. Schools.—Chap. X. Parochial lay co-operation.—Chap. XI Auxiliary
Parochial Institutions.—Chap. XII. Parish Festivals.—Chap. XIII. Mis-
cellaneous Responsibilities.

Blunt's (Rev. J. H.) Household Theology; a Handbook of
Religious Information respecting the Holy Bible, the Prayer Book, the
Church, the Ministry, Divine Worship, the Creeds, &c., &c. Small
8vo. 6s.

Boyle's (W. R. A.) Inspiration of the Book of Daniel, and other portions of Sacred Scripture. With a correction of Profane, and an adjustment of Sacred Chronology. 8vo. 14s.

Bright's (Rev. W.) Faith and Life ; Readings for the greater Holydays, and the Sundays from Advent to Trinity. Compiled from Ancient Writers. Small 8vo. 5s.

Brown's (Rev. G. J.) Lectures on the Gospel according to St. John, in the form of a Continuous Commentary. 2 vols. 8vo. 24s.

Browne's (Sir Thomas) Christian Morals. With a Life of the Author by Samuel Johnson. In small 8vo. with Portrait of Author, price 6s. handsomely printed on toned paper from antique type.

Burke.—A Complete Edition of the Works and Correspondence of the Right Hon. Edmund Burke. In 8 vols. 8vo. With Portrait. 4l. 4s.

> Contents :—1. Mr. Burke's Correspondence between the year 1744 and his Decease in 1797, first published from the original MSS. in 1844, edited by Earl Fitzwilliam and Sir Richard Bourke. The most interesting portion of the Letters of Mr. Burke to Dr. French Laurence is also included in it.
>
> 2. The Works of Mr. Burke, as edited by his Literary Executors, and completed by the publication of the 15th and 16th Volumes, in 1826, under the Superintendence of the late Bishop of Rochester, Dr. Walker King.

Burke's (Edmund) Reflections on the Revolution in France, in 1790. New Edition, with a short Biographical Notice. 8vo. 4s. 6d.

Cambridge Year-Book and University Almanack for 1865. Edited by William White, Sub-Librarian of Trinity College. Crown 8vo. 2s. 6d. sewed ; or, 3s. 6d. in cloth.

Caswall's (Rev. Dr.) Martyr of the Pongas. A Memoir of the Rev. Hamble James Leacock, first West-Indian Missionary to Western Africa. Small 8vo. With Portrait. 5s. 6d.

Chase's (Rev. D. P.) Translation of the Nicomachean Ethics of Aristotle ; with an Introduction, a Marginal Analysis, and Explanatory Notes. Designed for the use of Students in the Universities. Second Edition, revised. Crown 8vo. 6s.

Christian's (The) Duty, from the Sacred Scriptures. In Two Parts. Part I. Exhortation to Repentance and a Holy Life. Part II. Devotions for the Closet, in Three Offices, for every Day in the Week. [London : sold by C. Rivington, in St. Paul's Churchyard. 1730.] New Edition. Edited by the Rev. Thomas Dale, M.A. Small 8vo. (1852.) 5s.

Clarke's (Rev. B. S.) Essay towards the Interpretation of the Apocalypse; with Appendices on Ezekiel xl.—xlviii., and Plans. 8vo. 8s.

Clergy Charities.—List of Charities, General and Diocesan, for the Relief of the Clergy, their Widows and Families. Fifth Edition. Small 8vo. 3s.

Clissold's (Rev. H.) Lamps of the Church; or, Rays of Faith, Hope, and Charity, from the Lives and Deaths of some Eminent Christians of the Nineteenth Century. *New and cheaper Edition.* Crown 8vo., with five Portraits. 5s.

Codd's (Rev. A.) The Fifty-Third Chapter of Isaiah. A Course of Lectures, delivered in Holy Week and on Easter Day, in the Parish Church of Beaminster, Dorset. Small 8vo. 3s. 6d.

Cotterill's Selection of Psalms and Hymns for Public Worship. New and cheaper Editions. 32mo., 1s.; in 18mo. (large print), 1s. 6d. Also an Edition on fine paper, 2s. 6d.
   。 A large allowance to Clergymen and Churchwardens.

Cox's (Miss) Hymns from the German; accompanied by the German originals. Second Edition, elegantly printed in small 8vo. 5s.

Cox's (Rev. J. M.) The Church on the Rock: or, the Claims and some Distinctive Doctrines of the Church of Rome considered, in Six Lectures. Small 8vo. 3s.

Coxe's (Archdeacon) Plain Thoughts on Important Church Subjects. Small 8vo. 3s.

Crosthwaite's (Rev. J. C.) Historical Passages and Characters in the Book of Daniel; Eight Lectures, delivered in 1852, at the Lecture founded by the late Bernard Hyde, Esq. To which are added, Four Discourses on Mutual Recognition in a Future State. 12mo. 7s. 6d.

Daily Service Hymnal. 12mo., 1s. 6d. 32mo., 6d.

Davys's (Bp. of Peterborough) Plain and Short History of England for Children: in Letters from a Father to his Son. With Questions. Fourteenth and Cheaper Edition. 18mo. 1s. 6d.

Denton's (Rev. W.) Commentary, Practical and Exegetical, on the Lord's Prayer. Small 8vo. 5s.

Ellison's (Rev. H. J.) Way of Holiness in Married Life; a Course of Sermons preached in Lent. Second Edition. Small 8vo. 2s. 6d. *In white cloth, antique style, 3s. 6d.*

Espin's (Rev. T. E.) Critical Essays. Crown 8vo. 7s. 6d.
   Contents:—Wesleyan Methodism—Essays and Reviews—Edward Irving—Sunday—Bishop Wilson, of Sodor and Man—Bishop Wilson, of Calcutta—Calvin.

Evans's (Rev. R. W.) Bishopric of Souls. Fourth Edition. Small 8vo. 5s.

A 3

Evans's (Rev. R. W.) Ministry of the Body. Second Edition. Small 8vo. 6s. 6d.

Exton's (Rev. R. B.) Speculum Gregis; or, the Parochial Minister's Assistant in the Oversight of his Flock. With blank forms to be filled up at discretion. Seventh Edition. In pocket size. 4s. 6d. bound with clasp.

Fearon's (Rev. H.) Sermons on Public Subjects. Small 8vo. 3s. 6d.

Giles's (Rev. J. D.) Village Sermons preached at some of the chief Christian Seasons, in the Parish Church of Belleau with Aby. Small 8vo. 5s.

Gilly's (Rev. Canon) Memoir of Felix Neff, Pastor of the High Alps; and of his Labours among the French Protestants of Dauphiné, a Remnant of the Primitive Christians of Gaul. Sixth Edition. Fcap. 5s. 6d.

Girdlestone's (Rev. Charles) Holy Bible, containing the Old and New Testaments: with a Commentary arranged in Short Lectures for the Daily Use of Families. New Edition, in 6 vols. 8vo. 3l. 3s.
The Old Testament separately. 4 vols. 8vo. 42s.
The New Testament. 2 vols. 8vo. 21s.

Goulburn's (Rev. Dr.) Thoughts on Personal Religion. Seventh Edition. Small 8vo. 6s. 6d.

Goulburn's (Rev. Dr.) Office of the Holy Communion in the Book of Common Prayer: a Series of Lectures delivered in the Church of St. John the Evangelist, Paddington. Third Edition. Small 8vo. 6s.

Goulburn's (Rev. Dr.) Sermons preached on Various Occasions during the last Twenty Years. Second Edition. 2 vols. small 8vo. 10s. 6d.

Goulburn's (Rev. Dr.) Four Sermons on Subjects of the Day. Second Edition. 1s. 6d.

Goulburn's (Rev. Dr.) The Idle Word: Short Religious Essays upon the Gift of Speech, and its Employment in Conversation. Third Edition. Small 8vo. 3s.

Goulburn's (Rev. Dr.) Introduction to the Devotional Study of the Holy Scriptures. Seventh Edition. Small 8vo. 3s. 6d.

Goulburn's (Rev. Dr.) Family Prayers, arranged on the Liturgical Principle. Third Edition. Small 8vo. 3s.

Goulburn's (Rev. Dr.) Short Devotional Forms, compiled to meet the Exigencies of a Busy life. New Edition, elegantly printed in square 16mo. 1s. 6d.

Goulburn's (Rev. Dr.) Manual of Confirmation. Fifth Edition. 1s. 6d.

Greswell's (Rev. Edward) The Three Witnesses and the Threefold Cord; being the Testimony of the Natural Measures of Time, of the Primitive Civil Calendar, and of Antediluvian and Postdiluvian Tradition, on the Principal Questions of Fact in Sacred or Profane Antiquity. 8vo. 7s. 6d.

Greswell's (Rev. Edward) Objections to the Historical Character of the Pentateuch, in Part I. of Dr. Colenso's " Pentateuch and Book of Joshua," considered, and shown to be unfounded. 8vo. 5s.

Greswell's (Rev. Edward) Exposition of the Parables and of other Parts of the Gospels. 5 vols. (in 6 parts), 8vo. 3l. 12s.

Grotius de Veritate Religionis Christianæ. With English Notes and Illustrations, for the use of Students. By the Rev. J. E. Middleton, M.A., of Trinity College, Cambridge; Lecturer on Theology at St. Bees' College. Second Edition. 12mo. 6s.

Gurney's (Rev. J. H.) Sermons on the Acts of the Apostles. With a Preface by the Dean of Canterbury. Small 8vo. 7s.

Gurney's (Rev. J. H.) Sermons chiefly on Old Testament Histories, from Texts in the Sunday Lessons. Second Edition. 6s.

Gurney's (Rev. J. H.) Sermons on Texts from the Epistles and Gospels for Twenty Sundays. Second Edition. 6s.

Gurney's (Rev. J. H.) Miscellaneous Sermons. 6s. •

Hale's (Archdeacon) Proposals for the Extension of the Ministry in the Church of England, by the Revival of a lower order of Ministers, and by the Addition of Suffragan Bishops, made on several occasions. 8vo. 2s. 6d.

Hale's (Archdeacon) Sick Man's Guide to Acts of Faith, Patience. Charity, and Repentance. Extracted from Bishop Taylor's Holy Dying. In large print. Second Edition. 8vo. 3s.

Hall's (Rev. W. J.) Psalms and Hymns adapted to the Services of the Church of England ; with a Supplement of additional Hymns and Indices. In 8vo., 5s. 6d —18mo., 3s.—24mo., 1s. 6d.—24mo., limp cloth, 1s. 3d.—32mo., 1s.—32mo., limp, 8d. (The Supplement may be had separately.)

• A Prospectus of the above, with Specimens of Type, and farther particulars, may be had of the Publishers.

Hall's Selection of Psalms and Hymns ; with Accompanying Tunes, selected and arranged by John Foster, of Her Majesty's Chapels Royal. Crown 8vo., *limp cloth*, 2s. 6d. The Tunes only, 1s.

Hall's Selection. An Edition of the above Tunes for the Organ. Oblong 8vo. 7s. 6d.

Help and Comfort for the Sick Poor. By the Author of " Sickness : its Trials and Blessings." Fourth Edition, *in large print.* 1s., *or* 1s. 6d. *in cloth.*

A 4

Henley's (Hon. and Rev. R.) Sermons on the Beatitudes,
preached at St. Mary's Church, Putney. Small 8vo. 3s.

Henley's (Hon. and Rev. R.) The Prayer of Prayers.
Small 8vo. 4s. 6d.

Hessey's (Rev. Dr.) Biographies of the Kings of Judah:
Twelve Lectures. Crown 8vo. 6s. 6d.

Heygate's (Rev. W. E.) Care of the Soul; or, Sermons
on Points of Christian Prudence. 12mo. 5s. 6d.

Heygate's (Rev. W. E.) The Good Shepherd; or, Christ
the Pattern, Priest, and Pastor. 18mo. 3s. 6d.

Hodgson's (Chr.) Instructions for the Use of Candidates for
Holy Orders, and of the Parochial Clergy, as to Ordination, Licences,
Induction, Pluralities, Residence, &c. &c.; with Acts of Parliament relating to the above, and Forms to be used. Eighth Edition, revised and
corrected. 8vo. 12s.

Holden's (Rev. Geo.) Ordinance of Preaching investigated.
Small 8vo. 3s. 6d.

Holden's (Rev. Geo.) Christian Expositor; or, Practical
Guide to the Study of the New Testament. Intended for the use of
General Readers. Second Edition. 12mo. 12s.

Hook's (Dean) Book of Family Prayer. Seventh Edition,
revised and enlarged. 18mo. 2s.

Hook's (Dean) Private Prayers. Fifth Edition. 18mo. 2s.

Hook's (Dean) Dictionary of Ecclesiastical Biography.
8 vols. 12mo. 2l. 11s.

Hours (The) of the Passion; with Devotional Forms for
Private and Household Use. 12mo. 5s. in limp cloth, or 6s. in cloth,
red edges.

Hulton's (Rev. C. G.) Catechetical Help to Bishop Butler's
Analogy. Third Edition. Post 8vo. 4s. 6d.

Hymns and Poems for the Sick and Suffering; in connexion
with the Service for the Visitation of the Sick. Selected from
various Authors. Edited by the Rev. T. V. Fosbery, M.A., Vicar of
St. Giles's, Reading. Sixth Edition. 5s. 6d. in cloth, or 9s. 6d. in morocco.

Jackson's (Bp. of Lincoln) Six Sermons on the Christian
Character; preached in Lent. Seventh Edition. Small 8vo. 3s. 6d.

James's (Rev. Dr.) Comment upon the Collects appointed
to be used in the Church of England on Sundays and Holydays throughout the Year. Fifteenth Edition. 12mo. 5s.

James's (Rev. Dr.) Christian Watchfulness in the Prospect
of Sickness, Mourning, and Death. Eighth Edition. 12mo. 6s.
    Cheap Editions of these two works may be had, price 3s. each.

James's (Rev. Dr.) Evangelical Life, as seen in the Example of our Lord Jesus Christ. Second Edition. 12mo. 7s. 6d.

James's (Rev. Dr.) Devotional Comment on the Morn-
ing and Evening Services in the Book of Common Prayer, in a Series of
Plain Lectures. Second Edition. In 2 vols. 12mo. 10s. 6d.

Inman's (Rev. Professor) Treatise on Navigation and
Nautical Astronomy, for the Use of British Seamen. Thirteenth Edition,
edited by the Rev. J. W. Inman. Royal 8vo. 7s.

Inman's (Rev. Professor) Nautical Tables for the Use
of British Seamen. New Edition, edited by the Rev. J. W. Inman.
Royal 8vo. 14s.

Jones's (Rev. Harry) Life in the World: Sermons at St.
Luke's, Berwick Street. Small 8vo. 5s.

Kaye's (Bishop) Account of the Writings and Opinions
of Justin Martyr. Third Edition. 8vo. 7s. 6d.

Kaye's (Bishop) Ecclesiastical History of the Second and
Third Centuries, Illustrated from the Writings of Tertullian. Third
Edition. 8vo. 13s.

Kaye's (Bishop) Account of the Writings and Opinions of
Clement of Alexandria. 8vo. 12s.

Kaye's (Bishop) Account of the Council of Nicæa, in
connexion with the Life of Athanasius. 8vo. 8s.

Kennaway's (Rev. C. E.) Consolatio; or, Comfort for the
Afflicted. Selected from various Authors. With a Preface by the Bishop
of Oxford. Eleventh Edition. Small 8vo. 4s. 6d.

Knowles's (Rev. E. H.) Notes on the Epistle to the Hebrews, with Analysis and Brief Paraphrase; for Theological Students.
Crown 8vo. 6s. 6d.

Lee's (Archdeacon) Eight Discourses on the Inspiration of
Holy Scripture. Fourth Edition. 8vo. 15s.

Lee's (Rev. F. G.) The Words from the Cross: Seven Sermons for Lent and Passion-tide. Second Edition. Small 8vo. 2s. 6d.

Lewis's (Rev. W. S.) Threshold of Revelation; or, Some
Inquiry into the Province and True Character of the First Chapter of
Genesis. Crown 8vo. 6s.

London Diocese Book for 1865: containing an account of the
See and its Bishops; of St. Paul's Cathedral, Westminster Abbey, and
the Chapels Royal; of the Rural Deaneries, Foreign Chaplaincies, &c.
By John Hassard, Private Secretary to the Bishop of London. Second
Edition. Crown 8vo. 2s. 6d.

A 5

McCaul's (Rev. Dr.) Examination of Bp. Colenso's Difficulties with regard to the Pentateuch; and some Reasons for believing in its Authenticity and Divine Origin. Third Library Edition. Crown 8vo. 5s.

McCaul's (Rev. Dr.) Examination of Bp. Colenso's Difficulties with regard to the Pentateuch. Part II. Crown 8vo. 2s.

Mackenzie's (Rev. H.) Ordination Lectures, delivered in Riseholme Palace Chapel, during Ember Weeks. Small 8vo. 3s.

    Contents:—Pastoral Government—Educational Work—Self-government in the Pastor—Missions and their Reflex Results—Dissent—Public Teaching—Sunday Schools—Doctrinal Controversy—Secular Aids.

Maitland's (Rev. Dr.) Voluntary System; in a Series of Letters. 12mo. 6s. 6d.

Maitland's (Rev. Dr.) Dark Ages: a Series of Essays in illustration of the Religion and Literature of the Ninth, Tenth, Eleventh, and Twelfth Centuries. Third Edition. 8vo. 12s.

Maitland's (Rev. Dr.) Essays on Subjects connected with the Reformation in England. 8vo. 15s.

Mansel's (Rev. Professor) Artis Logicæ Rudimenta, from the Text of Aldrich; with Notes and Marginal References. Fourth Edition, corrected and enlarged. 8vo. 10s. 6d.

Mansel's (Rev. Professor) Prolegomena Logica; an Inquiry into the Psychological Character of Logical Processes. Second Edition. 8vo. 10s. 6d.

Mant's (Bishop) Book of Common Prayer and Administration of the Sacraments, with copious Notes, Practical and Historical, from approved Writers of the Church of England; including the Canons and Constitutions of the Church. New Edition. In one volume, super-royal 8vo. 24s.

Mant's (Bishop) Happiness of the Blessed considered as to the Particulars of their State; their Recognition of each other in that State; and its Difference of Degrees. Seventh Edition. 12mo. 4s.

Margaret Stourton; or, a Year of Governess Life. Elegantly printed in small 8vo. Price 5s.

Marriott's (Rev. Wharton B.) Adelphi of Terence, with English Notes. Small 8vo. 3s.

Marsh's (Bishop) Comparative View of the Churches of England and Rome: with an Appendix on Church Authority, the Character of Schism, and the Rock on which our Saviour declared that He would build His Church. Third Edition. Small 8vo. 6s.

Massingberd's (Rev. F. C.) Lectures on the Prayer-Book. Small 8vo. 3s. 6d.

Mayd's (Rev. W.) Sunday Evening; or, a Short and Plain Exposition of the Gospel for every Sunday in the Year. Crown 8vo. 5s.

Medd's (Rev. P. G.) Household Prayer; with Morning and Evening Readings for a Month. Small 8vo. 4s. 6d.

Melvill's (Rev. H.) Sermons. Vol. I., Sixth Edition. Vol. II., Fourth Edition. 10s. 6d. each.

Melvill's (Rev. H.) Sermons on some of the less prominent Facts and References in Sacred Story. Second Series. 8vo. 10s. 6d.

Melvill's (Rev. H.) Selection from the Lectures delivered at St. Margaret's, Lothbury, on the Tuesday Mornings in the Years 1850, 1851, 1852. Small 8vo. 6s.

Middleton's (Bp.) Doctrine of the Greek Article applied to the Criticism and Illustration of the New Testament. With Prefatory Observations and Notes, by Hugh James Rose, B.D., late Principal of King's College, London. New Edition. 8vo. 12s.

Mill's (Rev. Dr.) Analysis of Bishop Pearson on the Creed. Third Edition. 8vo. 5s.

Miller's (Rev. J. K.) Parochial Sermons. Small 8vo. 4s. 6d.

Missing Doctrine (The) in Popular Preaching. Small 8vo. 5s.

Monsell's (Rev. Dr.) Parish Musings; or, Devotional Poems. Eighth Edition, elegantly printed on toned paper. Small 8vo. 2s. 6d.

Also, a CHEAP EDITION, price 1s. sewed, or 1s. 6d. in limp cloth.

Moore's (Rev. Daniel) The Age and the Gospel; Four Sermons preached before the University of Cambridge, at the Hulsean Lecture, 1864. Crown 8vo. 5s.

Moreton's (Rev. Julian) Life and Work in Newfoundland: Reminiscences of Thirteen Years spent there. Crown 8vo., with a Map and four Illustrations. 5s. 6d.

Mozley's (Rev. J. B.) Review of the Baptismal Controversy. 8vo. 9s. 6d.

Nixon's (Bishop) Lectures, Historical, Doctrinal, and Practical, on the Catechism of the Church of England. Sixth Edition. 8vo. 18s.

Notes on Wild Flowers. By a Lady. Small 8vo. 9s.

Old Man's (The) Rambles. Sixth and cheaper Edition. 18mo. 3s. 6d.

A 6

Parkinson's (Canon) Old Church Clock. Fourth Edition.
Small 8vo. 4s. 6d.

Parry's (Mrs.) Young Christian's Sunday Evening; or,
Conversations on Scripture History. In 3 vols. small 8vo. Sold
separately:

First Series : on the Old Testament. Fourth Edition. 6s. 6d.
Second Series: on the Gospels. Third Edition. 7s.
Third Series: on the Acts. Second Edition. 4s. 6d.

Parry's (Rev. E. St. John) School Sermons preached at
Leamington College. Small 8vo. 4s. 6d.

Peile's (Rev. Dr.) Annotations on the Apostolical Epistles.
New Edition. 4 vols. 8vo. 42s.

Pepys's (Lady C.) Quiet Moments: a Four Weeks' Course
of Thoughts and Meditations before Evening Prayer and at Sunset.
Fourth Edition. Small 8vo. 3s. 6d.

Pepys's (Lady C.) Morning Notes of Praise: a Companion
Volume. Second Edition. 3s. 6d.

Pepys's (Lady C.) Thoughts for the Hurried and Hard-
working. Second Edition, in large print, price 1s. sewed, or 1s. 6d. in
limp cloth.

Physical Science compared with the Second Beast of the
Revelations. Small 8vo. 3s. 6d.

Pinder's (Rev. Canon) Sermons on the Book of Common
Prayer and Administration of the Sacraments. To which are now added,
Several Sermons on the Feasts and Fasts of the Church, preached in the
Cathedral Church of Wells. Third Edition. 12mo. 7s.

Pinder's (Rev. Canon) Sermons on the Holy Days observed
in the Church of England throughout the Year. Second Edition. 12mo.
6s. 6d.

Pinder's (Rev. Canon) Meditations and Prayers on the Ordi-
nation Service for Deacons. Small 8vo. 3s. 6d.

Pinder's (Rev. Canon) Meditations and Prayers on the Ordi-
nation Service for Priests. Small 8vo. 3s. 6d.

Plain Sermons. By Contributors to the "Tracts for the
Times." In 10 vols. 8vo., 6s. 6d. each. (Sold separately.)

This Series contains 347 original Sermons of moderate length, written
in simple language, and in an earnest and impressive style, forming a
copious body of practical Theology, in accordance with the Doctrines
of the Church of England. They are particularly suited for family reading.
The last Volume contains a general Index of Subjects, and a Table of
the Sermons adapted to the various Seasons of the Christian Year.

Prayers for the Sick and Dying. By the Author of "Sickness, its Trials and Blessings." Fourth Edition. Small 8vo. 2s. 6d.

Priest (The) to the Altar; or, Aids to the Devout Celebration of Holy Communion, chiefly after the Ancient English Use of Sarum. 8vo. 7s. 6d.

Public Schools (The) Calendar for 1865. Edited by a Graduate of the University of Oxford. Small 8vo. (pp, 570). 6s.

‗ This Work is intended to furnish Annually an account of the Foundations and Endowments of the Schools; of the Course of Study and Discipline; Scholarships and Exhibitions; Fees and other Expenses; School Prizes and University Honours; Recreations and Vacations; Religious Instruction; and other useful information.

Pusey's (Rev. Dr.) Commentary on the Minor Prophets: with Introductions to the several Books. In 4to.
Parts I., II., III., price 5s. each, are already published.

Pusey's (Rev. Dr.) Daniel the Prophet; Nine Lectures delivered in the Divinity School. Third Thousand. 8vo. 12s.

Ramsay (Dean) on Christian Responsibility. Small 8vo. 3s. 6d.

Reminiscences by a Clergyman's Wife. Edited by the Dean of Canterbury. Second Edition. Crown 8vo. 3s. 6d.

Schmitz's (Dr. L.) Manual of Ancient History, from the Remotest Times to the Overthrow of the Western Empire, A.D. 476. Third Edition. Crown 8vo. 7s. 6d.

This Work, for the convenience of Schools, may be had in Two Parts, sold separately, viz.:—
Vol. I., containing, besides the History of India and the other Asiatic Nations, a complete History of Greece. 4s.
Vol. II., containing a complete History of Rome. 4s.

Schmitz's (Dr. L.) Manual of Ancient Geography. Crown 8vo. 6s.

Schmitz's (Dr. L.) History of the Middle Ages, from the Downfall of the Western Empire, A.D. 476, to the Crusades, A.D. 1096. Crown 8vo. 7s. 6d.

Scripture Record of the Life and Times of Samuel the Prophet. By the Author of "Scripture Record of the Blessed Virgin." Small 8vo. 3s.

Seymour's (Rev. R.) and Mackarness's (Rev. J. F.) Eighteen Years of a Clerical Meeting: being the Minutes of the Alcester Clerical Association, from 1842 to 1860; with a Preface on the Revival of Ruridecanal Chapters. Crown 8vo. 6s. 6d.

Sickness, its Trials and Blessings. Seventh Edition. Small 8vo. 3s. 6d. Also, a cheaper Edition, for distribution, 2s. 6d.

Slade's (Rev. Canon) Twenty-one Prayers composed from
the Psalms for the Sick and Afflicted: with other Forms of Prayer, and
Hints and Directions for the Visitation of the Sick. Seventh Edition.
12mo. 3s. 6d.

Slade's (Rev. Canon) Plain Parochial Sermons. 7 vols. 12mo.
6s. each. Sold separately.

Smith's (Rev. J. G.) Life of Our Blessed Saviour: an
Epitome of the Gospel Narrative, arranged in order of time from the latest
Harmonics. With Introduction and Notes. Square 16mo. 2s.

Smith's (Rev. Dr. J. B.) Manual of the Rudiments of
Theology: containing an Abridgment of Tomline's Elements; an Analysis
of Paley's Evidences; a Summary of Pearson on the Creed; and a brief
Exposition of the Thirty-nine Articles, chiefly from Burnet; Explanation
of Jewish Rites and Ceremonies, &c. &c. Fifth Edition. 12mo. 8s. 6d.

Smith's (Rev. Dr. J. B.) Compendium of Rudiments in
Theology: containing a Digest of Bishop Butler's Analogy; an Epitome
of Dean Graves on the Pentateuch; and an Analysis of Bishop Newton
on the Prophecies. Second Edition. 12mo. 9s.

Talbot's (Hon. Mrs. J. C.) Parochial Mission-Women; their
Work and its Fruits. Second Edition. Small 8vo. *In limp cloth*, 2s.

Thornton's (Rev. T.) Life of Moses, in a Course of Village
Lectures; with a Preface Critical of Bishop Colenso's Work on the
Pentateuch. Small 8vo. 3s. 6d.

Threshold (The) of Private Devotion. Second Edition.
18mo. 2s.

Townsend's (Canon) Holy Bible, containing the Old and
New Testaments, arranged in Historical and Chronological Order. With
copious Notes and Indexes. Fifth Edition. In 2 vols., imperial 8vo.,
21s. *each* (sold separately).
    Also, an Edition of this Arrangement of the Bible without the Notes,
in One Volume, 14s.

Trollope's (Rev. W.) Iliad of Homer from a carefully corrected Text; with copious English Notes, illustrating the Grammatical
Construction, the Manners and Customs, the Mythology and Antiquities
of the Heroic Ages; and Preliminary Observations on points of Classical
interest. Fifth Edition. 8vo. 15s.

Trollope's (Rev. W.) Excerpta ex Ovidii Metam. et Epistolæ.
With English Notes, and an Introduction, containing Rules for Construing, a Parsing Praxis, &c. Third Edition. 12mo. 3s. 6d.

Trollope's (Rev. W.) Bellum Catilinarium of Sallust, and
Cicero's Four Orations against Catiline; with English Notes and Intro-
duction. Together with the Bellum Jugurthinum of Sallust. Third
Edition. 12mo. 3s. 6d.

Truth without Prejudice. Fourth Edition. Small 8vo. 3s. 6d.

Tyler's (Rev. O. B.) Doctrine and Practice of the Christian
Life, in a Series of Sermons. Second Edition. Small 8vo. 3s. 6d.

Vidal's (Mrs.) Tales for the Bush. Originally published in
Australia. Fourth Edition. Small 8vo. 5s.

Virgilii Æneidos Libri I—VI; with English Notes, chiefly
from the Edition of P. Wagner, by T. Clayton, M.A., and C. S. Jerram,
M.A. Small 8vo. 4s. 6d.

Warter's (Rev. J. W.) The Sea-board and the Down; or,
My Parish in the South. In 2 vols. small 4to. Elegantly printed in
Antique type, with Illustrations. 28s.

Webster's (Rev. W.) Syntax and Synonyms of the Greek
Testament. 8vo. 9s.

The Syntax is based upon Donald-son's, with extracts from the writings of Archbishop Trench, Dean Alford, Dr. Wordsworth, but more especially from Bishop Ellicott, and the work on the Romans by Dr. Vaughan. Considerable use has also been made of the Article in the "Quarterly Review" for January, 1863.

The chapter on Synonyms treats of many words which have not been noticed by other writers. In another chapter attention is drawn to some passages in which the Authorized Version is incorrect, inexact, insufficient, or obscure. Copious Indices are added.

Welchman's Thirty-nine Articles of the Church of England,
illustrated with Notes. New Edition. 2s. Or, interleaved with blank
paper, 3s.

Wilberforce's (Bp. of Oxford) History of the Protestant
Episcopal Church in America. Third Edition. Small 8vo. 5s.

Wilberforce's (Bp. of Oxford) Rocky Island, and other Simi-
litudes. Twelfth Edition, with Cuts. 18mo. 2s. 6d.

Wilberforce's (Bp. of Oxford) Sermons preached before the
Queen. Sixth Edition. 12mo. 6s.

Wilberforce's (Bp. of Oxford) Selection of Psalms and Hymns
for Public Worship. New Edition. 32mo. 1s. each, or 3l. 10s. per hundred.

Williams's (Rev. Isaac) The Psalms interpreted of Christ;
a Devotional Commentary. Vol. I. Small 8vo. 7s. 6d.

Williams's (Rev. Isaac) Devotional Commentary on the
Gospel Narrative. 8 vols. small 8vo. 3l. 6s.

Sold separately as follows :—

Thoughts on the Study of the Gospels. 8s.
Harmony of the Evangelists. 8s. 6d.
The Nativity (extending to the Calling of St. Matthew). 8s. 6d.
Second Year of the Ministry. 8s.
Third Year of the Ministry. 8s. 6d.
The Holy Week. 8s. 6d.   The Passion. 8s.
The Resurrection. 8s.

Williams's (Rev. Isaac) Apocalypse, with Notes and Reflections. Small 8vo. 8s. 6d.

Williams's (Rev. Isaac) Beginning of the Book of Genesis, with Notes and Reflections. Small 8vo. 7s. 6d.

Williams's (Rev. Isaac) Sermons on the Characters of the Old Testament. Second Edition. 5s. 6d.

Williams's (Rev. Isaac) Female Characters of Holy Scripture; in a Series of Sermons. Second Edition. Small 8vo. 5s. 6d.

Williams's (Rev. Isaac) Plain Sermons on the Latter Part of the Catechism; being the Conclusion of the Series contained in the Ninth Volume of "Plain Sermons." 8vo. 6s. 6d.

Williams's (Rev. Isaac) Complete Series of Sermons on the Catechism. In one Volume. 13s.

Williams's (Rev. Isaac) Sermons on the Epistle and Gospel for the Sundays and Holy Days throughout the Year. Second Edition. In 3 vols. small 8vo. 16s. 6d.

     ₊ The Third Volume, on the Saints' Days and other Holy Days of the Church, may be had separately, price 5s. 6d.

Williams's (Rev. Isaac) Christian Seasons; a Series of Poems. Small 8vo. 3s. 6d.

Wilson's (Rev. Plumpton) Meditations and Prayers for Persons in Private. Fourth Edition, elegantly printed in 18mo. 4s. 6d.

Wilson's (late Bp. of Sodor and Man) Short and Plain Instruction for the Better Understanding of the Lord's Supper. To which is annexed, The Office of the Holy Communion, with Proper Helps and Directions. Pocket size, 1s. Also, a larger Edition, 2s.

Wilson's (late Bp. of Sodor and Man) Sacra Privata; Private Meditations and Prayers. Pocket size, 1s. Also, a larger Edition, 2s.

     These two Works may be had in various bindings.

Woodward's (Rev. F. B.) Tracts and Sermons on Subjects of the Day; with an Appendix on the Roman Catholic Controversy. 12mo. 7s.

Wordsworth's (late Rev. Dr.) Ecclesiastical Biography; or, Lives of Eminent Men connected with the History of Religion in England, from the Commencement of the Reformation to the Revolution. Selected, and Illustrated with Notes. Fourth Edition. In 4 vols. 8vo. With 5 Portraits. 2l. 14s.

Wordsworth's (Bp. of St. Andrew's) Christian Boyhood at a Public School: a Collection of Sermons and Lectures delivered at Winchester College from 1836 to 1846. In 2 vols. 8vo. 1l. 4s.

Wordsworth's (Bp. of St. Andrew's) Catechesis; or, Christian Instruction preparatory to Confirmation and First Communion. Third Edition. Crown 8vo. 3s. 6d.

Wordsworth's (Archd.) New Testament of our Lord and Saviour Jesus Christ, in the original Greek. With Notes, Introductions, and Indexes. New Edition. In Two Vols., imperial 8vo. 4l.

Separately,

Part I.: The Four Gospels. 1l. 1s.
Part II.: The Acts of the Apostles. 10s. 6d.
Part III.: The Epistles of St. Paul. 1l. 11s. 6d.
Part IV.: The General Epistles and Book of Revelation; with Indexes. 1l. 1s.

Wordsworth's (Archd.) The Holy Bible. With Notes and Introductions. Part I., containing Genesis and Exodus. Imperial 8vo. 21s. Part II., Leviticus to Deuteronomy. 18s.

Wordsworth's (Archd.) Occasional Sermons preached in Westminster Abbey. In 7 vols. 8vo. Vols. I., II., and III., 7s. each— Vols. IV. and V., 8s. each—Vol. VI., 7s.—Vol. VII., 6s.

Wordsworth's (Archd.) Theophilus Anglicanus; or, Instruction concerning the Principles of the Church Universal and the Church of England. New Edition. 5s.

Wordsworth's (Archd.) Elements of Instruction on the Church; being an Abridgment of the above. Second Edition. 2s.

Wordsworth's (Archd.) Journal of a Tour in Italy; with Reflections on the Present Condition and Prospects of Religion in that Country. Second Edition. 2 vols. post 8vo. 15s.

Wordsworth's (Archd.) On the Interpretation of the Bible. Five Lectures delivered at Westminster Abbey. 3s. 6d.

Wordsworth's (Archd.) Holy Year: Hymns for Sundays and Holydays, and for other Occasions; with a preface on Hymnology. Third Edition, in larger type, square 16mo., cloth extra, 4s. 6d. Also an Edition with Tunes, 4s. 6d.; and a cheap Edition, 6d.

Worgan's (Rev. J. H.) Divine Week; or, Outlines of a Harmony of the Geologic Periods with the Mosaic "Days" of Creation. Crown 8vo. 5s.

Yonge's (C. D.) History of England from the Earliest Times to the Peace of Paris, 1856. With a Chronological Table of Contents. In one thick volume, crown 8vo. 12s.

Though available as a School-book, this volume contains as much as three ordinary octavos. It is written on a carefully digested plan, ample space being given to the last three centuries. All the best authorities have been consulted.

A

SELECTION FROM THE SCHOOL SERIES

OF THE

REV. THOMAS KERCHEVER ARNOLD, M.A.

LATE FELLOW OF TRINITY COLLEGE, CAMBRIDGE.

Practical Introductions to Greek, Latin, &c.

Henry's First Latin Book. Eighteenth Edition. 12mo. 3s.

The object of this work is to enable the youngest boys to master the principal difficulties of the Latin language by easy steps, and to furnish older students with a Manual for Self-Tuition.

Great attention has lately been given to the improvement of what may be called its mechanical parts. The Vocabularies have been much extended, and greater uniformity of reference has been secured. A few rules have been omitted or simplified. Every thing has been done which the long experience of the Editor, or the practice of his friends in their own schools has shown to be desirable.

At the same time, no pains have been spared to do this without altering in any way the character of the work, or making it inconvenient to use it side by side with copies of earlier editions.

** *A small book of* SUPPLEMENTARY EXERCISES *is in the press.*

A Second Latin Book, and Practical Grammar. Intended as a Sequel to Henry's First Latin Book. Eighth Edition. 12mo. 4s.

A First Verse Book, Part I. ; intended as an easy Introduction to the Latin Hexameter and Pentameter. Eighth Edition. 12mo. 2s.

A First Verse Book, Part II. ; containing additional Exercises. Second Edition. 1s.

Historiæ Antiquæ Epitome, from *Cornelius Nepos, Justin,* &c. With English Notes, Rules for Construing, Questions, Geographical Lists, &c. Seventh Edition. 4s.

A First Classical Atlas, containing fifteen Maps, coloured in outline; intended as a Companion to the *Historiæ Antiquæ Epitome.* 8vo. 7s. 6d.

A Practical Introduction to Latin Prose Composition. Part I. Thirteenth Edition. 8vo. 6s. 6d.

This Work is founded on the principles of imitation and frequent repetition. It is at once a Syntax, a Vocabulary, and an Exercise Book; and considerable attention has been paid to the subject of Synonymes. It is now used at all, or nearly all, the public schools.

A Practical Introduction to Latin Prose Composition, Part II.; containing the Doctrine of Latin Particles, with Vocabulary, an Antibarbarus, &c. Fourth Edition. 8vo. 8s.

A Practical Introduction to Latin Verse Composition. Fourth and Cheaper Edition, considerably revised. 12mo. 3s. 6d.

> This Work supposes the pupil to be already capable of composing verses easily when the "*full sense*" is given. Its object is to facilitate his transition to original composition in Elegiacs and Hexameters, and to teach him to compose the Alcaic and Sapphic stanzas: explanations and a few exercises are also given on the other Horatian metres. A short Poetical Phraseology is added.
>
> In the present Edition the whole work has been corrected, the translations being carefully compared with the originals. The Alcaics and Sapphics have been arranged in stanzas, and each kind of verse placed in a separate chapter, the old numbers of the Exercises being preserved for convenience in use. Other improvements have been made which it is hoped will add to its value.

Gradus ad Parnassum Novus Anticlepticus; founded on Quicherat's *Thesaurus Poeticus Linguæ Latinæ*. 8vo. *half-bound.* 10s. 6d.

⁎⁎* A Prospectus, with specimen page, may be had of the Publishers.

Longer Latin Exercises, Part I. Third Edition. 8vo. 4s.

> The object of this Work is to supply boys with an easy collection of *short* passages, as an Exercise Book for those who have gone once, at least, through the First Part of the Editor's "Practical Introduction to Latin Prose Composition."

Longer Latin Exercises, Part II.; containing a Selection of Passages of greater length, in genuine idiomatic English, for Translation into Latin. 8vo. 4s.

Materials for Translation into Latin: selected and arranged by Augustus Grotefend. Translated from the German by the Rev. H. H. Arnold, B.A., with Notes and Excursuses. Third Edition. 8vo. 7s. 6d.

A Copious and Critical English-Latin Lexicon, by the Rev. T. K. Arnold and the Rev. J. E. Riddle. Sixth Edition. 1l. 5s.

An Abridgment of the above Work, for the Use of Schools. By the Rev J. C. Elden, late Fellow and Tutor of Trinity Hall, Cambridge. Square 12mo. *bound.* 10s. 6d.

The First Greek Book; on the Plan of "Henry's First Latin Book." Fifth Edition. 12mo. 5s.

The Second Greek Book (on the same Plan); containing an Elementary Treatise on the Greek Particles and the Formation of Greek Derivatives. 12mo. 5s. 6d.

A Practical Introduction to Greek Accidence. With Easy
Exercises and Vocabulary. Seventh Edition. 8vo. 5s. 6d.

A Practical Introduction to Greek Prose Composition, Part I.
Tenth Edition. 8vo. 5s. 6d.

The object of this Work is to enable the Student, as soon as he can
decline and conjugate with tolerable facility, to translate simple sentences
after given examples, and with given words; the principles trusted to
being principally those of *imitation and very frequent repetition*. It is at
once a Syntax, a Vocabulary, and an Exercise Book.

Professor Madvig's Syntax of the Greek Language, especially
of the Attic Dialect; translated by the Rev. Henry Browne, M.A.
Together with an Appendix on the Greek Particles; by the Translator.
Square 8vo. 8s. 6d.

An Elementary Greek Grammar. 12mo. 5s.; or, with
Dialects, 6s.

A Complete Greek and English Lexicon for the Poems of
Homer, and the Homeridæ. Translated from the German of Crusius,
by Professor Smith. New and Revised Edition. 9s. half-bound.

₊ A Prospectus and specimen of this Lexicon may be had.

A Copious Phraseological English-Greek Lexicon, founded
on a work prepared by J. W. Frädersdorff, Ph. Dr. of the Taylor-Institu-
tion, Oxford. Revised, Enlarged, and Improved by the Rev. T. K. Arnold,
M.A., formerly Fellow of Trinity College, Cambridge, and Henry Browne,
M.A., Vicar of Pevensey, and Prebendary of Chichester. Third Edition,
corrected, with the Appendix incorporated. 8vo. 21s.

₊ A Prospectus, with specimen page, may be had.

Classical Examination Papers. A Series of 93 Extracts
from Greek, Roman, and English Classics for Translation, with occasional
Questions and Notes; each extract on a separate leaf. Price of the whole
in a specimen packet, 4s., or six copies of any Separate Paper may be had
for 3d.

Keys to the following may be had by Tutors only:

First Latin Book, 1s.   Second Latin Book, 2s.
Cornelius Nepos, 1s.
First Verse Book, 1s.   Latin Verse Composition, 2s.
Latin Prose Composition, Parts I. and II., 1s. 6d. each.
Longer Latin Exercises, Part I., 1s. 6d.   Part II., 2s. 6d.
Greek Prose Composition, Part I., 1s. 6d.   Part II., 4s. 6d.
First Greek Book, 1s. 6d.   Second, 2s.

The First Hebrew Book; on the Plan of "Henry's First Latin Book." 12mo. Second Edition. 7s. 6d.   The Key. Second Edition. 3s. 6d.

The Second Hebrew Book, containing the Book of Genesis; together with a Hebrew Syntax, and a Vocabulary and Grammatical Commentary. 9s.

The First German Book; on the Plan of "Henry's First Latin Book." By the Rev. T. K. Arnold and Dr. Frädersdorff. Fifth Edition. 12mo. 5s. 6d.   The Key, 2s. 6d.

A Reading Companion to the First German Book; containing Extracts from the best Authors with a Vocabulary and Notes. 12mo. Second Edition. 4s.

The First French Book; on the Plan of "Henry's First Latin Book." Fifth Edition. 12mo. 5s. 6d.   Key to the Exercises, by Delille, 2s. 6d.

Henry's English Grammar; a Manual for Beginners. 12mo. 3s. 6d.

Spelling turned Etymology. Second Edition. 12mo. 2s. 6d.

The Pupil's Book, (a Companion to the above,) 1s. 3d.

Latin viâ English; being the Second Part of the above Work. Second Edition. 12mo. 4s. 6d.

An English Grammar for Classical Schools; being a Practical Introduction to "English Prose Composition." Sixth Edition. 12mo. 4s. 6d.

Handbooks for the Classical Student, with Questions.

Ancient History and Geography. Translated from the German of Pütz, by the Ven. Archdeacon Paul. Second Edition. 12mo. 6s. 6d.

Mediæval History and Geography. Translated from the German of Pütz. By the same. 12mo. 4s. 6d.

Modern History and Geography. Translated from the German of Pütz. By the same. 12mo. 5s. 6d.

Grecian Antiquities. By Professor Bojesen. Translated from the German Version of Dr. Hoffa. By the same. Second Edition. 12mo. 3*s*. 6*d*.

Roman Antiquities. By Professor Bojesen. Second Edition. 3*s*. 6*d*.

Hebrew Antiquities. By the Rev. Henry Browne, M.A. Prebendary of Chichester. 12mo. 4*s*.

*** This Work describes the manners and customs of the ancient Hebrews which were common to them with other nations, and the rites and ordinances which distinguished them as the chosen people Israel.

Greek Synonymes. From the French of Pillon. 6*s*. 6*d*.

Latin Synonymes. From the German of Döderlein. Translated by the Rev. H. H. Arnold. Second Edition. 4*s*.

Arnold's School Classics.

Cornelius Nepos, Part I.; with Critical Questions and Answers, and an imitative Exercise on each Chapter. Fourth Edition. 12mo. 4*s*.

Eclogæ Ovidianæ, with English Notes; Part I. (from the Elegiac Poems.) Tenth Edition. 12mo. 2*s*. 6*d*.

Eclogæ Ovidianæ, Part II. (from the Metamorphoses.) 5*s*.

The Æneid of Virgil, with English Notes. 12mo. 6*s*.

The Works of Horace, followed by English Introductions and Notes, adapted for School use. 12mo. 7*s*.

Cicero.—Selections from his Orations, with English Notes, from the best and most recent sources. Contents:—The Fourth Book of the Impeachment of Verres, the Four Speeches against Catiline, and the Speech for the Poet Archias. Second Edition. 12mo. 4*s*.

Cicero, Part II.; containing Selections from his Epistles, arranged in the order of time, with Accounts of the Consuls, Events of each year, &c. With English Notes from the best Commentators, especially Matthiæ. 12mo. 5*s*.

Cicero, Part III.; containing the Tusculan Disputations (entire). With English Notes from Tischer, by the Rev. Archdeacon Paul. Second Edition. 5*s*. 6*d*.

Cicero, Part IV.; containing De Finibus Malorum et Bonorum. (On the Supreme Good.) With a Preface, English Notes, &c., partly from Madvig and others, by the Rev James Beaven, D.D., late Professor of Theology in King's College, Toronto. 12mo. 5*s*. 6*d*.

Cicero, Part V. ; containing Cato Major, sive De Senectute
Dialogue; with English Notes from Sommerbrodt, by the Rev. Henry
Browne, M.A., Canon of Chichester. 12mo. 2s. 6d.

Homer for Beginners.—The First Three Books of the Iliad,
with English Notes; forming a sufficient Commentary for Young Students.
Third Edition. 12mo. 3s. 6d.

Homer. — The Iliad Complete, with English Notes and
Grammatical References. Third Edition. In one thick volume, 12mo.
half-bound 12s.
In this Edition, the Argument of each Book is divided into short Sec-
tions, which are prefixed to those portions of the Text, respectively, which
they describe. The Notes (principally from Dübner) are at the foot of
each page. At the end of the volume are useful Appendices.

Homer.—The Iliad, Books I. to IV. ; with a Critical Introduction, and copious English Notes. Second Edition. 12mo. 7s. 6d.

Demosthenes, with English Notes from the best and most
recent sources, Sauppe, Doberenz. Jacobs, Dissen, Westermann, &c.
The Olynthiac Orations   Second Edition. 12mo. 3s.
The Oration on the Crown. Second Edition. 12mo. 4s. 6d.
The Philippic Orations. Second Edition. 12mo. 4s.

Æschines.—Speech against Ctesiphon. 12mo. 4s.
The Text is that of Bailer and Sauppe; the Notes are by Professor
Champlin, with additional Notes by President Woolsey and the Editor.

Sophocles, with English Notes, from Schneidewin. By the
Ven Archdeacon Paul, and the Rev Henry Browne, M.A.
The Ajax. 3s.—The Philoctetes. 3s —The Œdipus Tyrannus. 4s.—
The Œdipus Coloneus 4s.—The Antigone. 4s.

Euripides, with English Notes, from Hartung, Dübner,
Witzschel, Schöne, &c.
The Hecuba.—The Hippolytus.—The Bacchæ.—The Medea.—The
Iphigenia in Tauris, 3s. each.

Aristophanes.—Eclogæ Aristophanicæ, with English Notes,
by Professor Felton. Part 1. (The Clouds.) 12mo. 3s. 6d. Part II.
(The Birds.) 3s. 6d.
₊ In this Edition the objectionable passages are omitted.

A Descriptive Catalogue of the whole of Arnold's School
Series, may be had gratis.
Also, Rivington's complete Classified School Catalogue.

Publishing Monthly, price 1s.

The Englishman's Magazine

OF

LITERATURE, RELIGION, SCIENCE, AND ART.

Contents of No. 6, for June, 1865.

Vol. I., January to June, 1865, price 7s. 6d., is now ready.

RIVINGTONS,

LONDON, OXFORD, AND CAMBRIDGE.